Knowing

God

Intimately

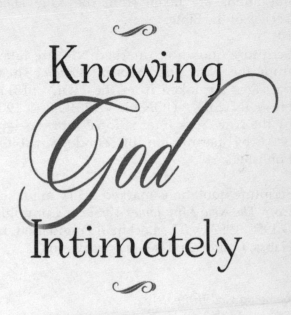

Knowing God Intimately

Clift & Kathleen Richards

Victory House, Inc.
Tulsa, Oklahoma

Unless otherwise indicated, all Scripture quotations are taken from the *King James Version* of the Bible.

Scripture quotations marked NIV are taken from the *New International Version*. Those passages are taken from the HOLY BIBLE: NEW INTERNATIONAL VERSION © 1978 by the New York International Bible Society, used by permission of Zondervan Bible Publishers.

Scripture quotations marked NKJV are taken from *The New King James Version*. Copyright © 1958, 1987 by The Lockman Foundation, La Habra, California. Used by permission.

CONTENTS

ACKNOWLEDGMENTS

The authors wish to acknowledge the capable assistance of their editor, Lloyd Hildebrand, and the staff at Victory House for their hard work, encouragement, and insightful contributions.

Books of Interest from Victory House

Prayer Keys
Breakthrough Prayers for Women
Prayers That Prevail
Prayers That Prevail for Your Children
More Prayers That Prevail
Mini Prayers That Prevail
Bible Prayers for All Your Needs
Praying Bible Promises
Believers' Prayers and Promises
God's Special Promises to Me
Today God Says **(Daily Devotional)**

Available at Your Christian Bookstore
or
from Victory House

INTRODUCTION

The Westminster Catechism, developed by British Protestants in 1646 as a spiritual aid to clergymen and children as well, clearly explains why knowing God is life's most important undertaking: "The chief end of man is to glorify God, and to enjoy Him forever." Truly, this is the overarching goal of life; it is the reason why we were created, and *Knowing God Intimately* is written with this end in mind – to help you comprehend and fulfill the purpose for which you were created.

God wants us to know Him intimately and personally, and by examining His personality and His attributes we are able to see Him as He really is. *Knowing God Intimately* leads us closer to the One who promises, "Draw near to God and He will draw near to you" (James 4:8, NKJV). The word "know," as it appears in the Bible, frequently presents the concept of an intimate and personal relationship. This goes far beyond the usual understanding of the word "know," which is often interpreted as meaning simply "to have information about or knowledge of."

There is a vast difference between knowing about God and actually knowing Him, or having a personal relationship with Him. *Knowing God Intimately* is written for everyone who seeks God, desires to serve Him and, above all else, wants to know Him both as the glorious Creator and as their own loving heavenly Father. To know Him in the way He desires is to experience Him in all of His power, glory, and love. It is also to experience life in a vibrant, joyful abundance that can barely be imagined apart from Him, and cannot be experienced in any other way.

We get to know God through a multitude of resources and experiences. In *Knowing God Intimately*, we discover some of the wonderful avenues to a deep, personal, abiding fellowship with the One who is both our King and our Father. However, this is not an easy journey. There are many barriers and pitfalls to avoid along the way.

Knowing God Intimately addresses these obstacles, and provides biblical ways to overcome them. It shows you how to enjoy fellowship with your heavenly Father through His Word, His grace, Jesus, His people, worship, His love, His power, His glory, nature, circumstances, the Holy Spirit, prayer, trust, praise, the blood of Jesus, His forgiveness, and many other ways.

The Bible gives us countless glimpses into the heart and personality of God so that we can get to know Him better. For example, the Bible tells us:

> *He is the God of our fathers in the faith.*
> *(See Exod. 3:6.)*
> *He is the God of the here-and-now.*
> *(See Exod. 3:14.)*
> *He is our Lord. (See Exod. 6:2.)*
> *He is our praise. (See Deut. 10:21.)*
> *He is our life and the length of our days.*
> *(See Deut. 30:20.)*
> *He is our Rock. (See Deut. 32:4.)*
> *He is eternal. (See Ps. 9:7.)*
> *His way is perfect. (See Ps. 18:30.)*
> *He is our Father. (See Ps. 89:26.)*
> *He is our Creator. (See Eccles. 12:1.)*
> *He is our Judge. (See Isa. 33:22.)*
> *He is our Savior and Redeemer.*
> *(See Isa. 60:16.)*
> *He is the true and living God.*
> *(See Jer. 10:10.)*
> *He is the fountain of living waters.*
> *(See Jer. 17:13.)*
> *He is righteous. (See Dan. 9:14.)*
> *He never changes. (See Mal. 3:6.)*
> *He is true. (See John 3:33.)*
> *He gives us life. (See Acts 17:25.)*
> *He is generous. (See Rom. 10:12.)*
> *He is powerful. (See Rom. 13:1.)*
> *He is faithful. (See 1 Thess. 5:24.)*
> *His foundation is sure. (See 2 Tim. 2:19.)*

> *He is our Rewarder. (See Heb. 11:6.)*
> *He is light. (See 1 John 1:5.)*
> *He is love. (See 1 John 4:8.)*
> *He is holy. (See Rev. 4:8.)*

These are but a few of the roles, activities, and attributes of our God. *Knowing God Intimately* covers all of these, plus many more. This book introduces you to God in all of His glory so that you can get to know Him better.

It is our hope that, as you travel with us through the pages of *Knowing God Intimately*, you will have an ever-increasing sense of His wonderful presence, His unconditional love, His uncompromising holiness, and His awesome power, majesty, and glory. So, let the journey begin.

Preface
THE FIRST STEPS TO TAKE IN KNOWING GOD

*For God so loved the world
that He gave His only begotten Son,
that whoever believes in Him
should not perish but have everlasting life.*
(John 3:16, NKJV)

God, who loves you, wants you to accept Jesus Christ, His Son, as your Savior and Lord. Why? Because that is the way of escape He has made for you out of the bondage of sin and death, and into a life that is glorious and eternal.

If you have already made a personal commitment to Christ, please take this opportunity to pray for the readers who need to know Jesus Christ as their personal Savior, and continue to read.

What does it mean to accept Jesus Christ as your Savior and Lord? It is so simple, and yet so profound. First, it means we must see ourselves as we really are: fallen from the estate in which our Creator intended us to live and, without Him, lost in sinfulness. No one is exempt from this horrible predicament. The Bible says, "For all have sinned, and come short of the glory of God" (Rom. 3:23). The price of sin is eternal death, as the Bible declares: "For the wages of sin is death, but the gift of God is eternal life in Christ Jesus our Lord" (Rom. 6:23, NKJV).

Jesus said, "Except a man be born again, he cannot see the kingdom of God" (John 3:3). In order to understand this, we must see Jesus as He really is. He said, "I am the way, the truth, and the life: no man cometh unto the Father, but by me" (John 14:6).

The key essential is belief. Believing in Jesus does not simply involve a mental assent to given facts or concepts, but it requires a willingness to put complete trust in Him — the object of your belief. To believe in Jesus, therefore, is to place your utmost trust and confidence in Him as your Savior and Lord.

In order to know God, you must repent of your sins. This simply means that you are sorry for your wrongdoings, and you want to turn away from each of your sins. Repentance will lead you to confess your sins to your heavenly Father who promises to forgive you. "If we confess our sins, He is faithful and just to forgive us our sins and to cleanse us from all unrighteousness" (1 John 1:9, NKJV).

You are about to discover that believing in Jesus Christ will revolutionize your life! You are on the threshold of the most exciting adventure you could ever have, one that will lead you into the most wonderful relationship of your life.

When you come to the realization and acceptance of God's plan, and have taken the steps of belief and repentance required, you will enter into an entirely new sphere of existence. Paul writes, "Therefore if any man be in Christ, he is a new creature; old things are passed away; behold, all things are become new. And all things are of God, who hath reconciled us to himself by Jesus Christ" (2 Cor. 5:17-18).

This passage describes what happens as a result of the new birth God offers to you. You are no longer condemned to eternal death and separation from God because of your sin. Now, you are legally God's child, a joint-heir with His Son, Jesus Christ, and you have been set free from the law of sin and death.

To accept Jesus as your Savior, then, is to see yourself as a sinner, to repent of your sins, and to submit your will and life to the Lordship of Christ. When you do this, God will see you through the righteousness of Christ, just as though you had never sinned.

He will see you as being pure and holy, like His Son, because He will see you *in* Jesus.

The Bible says, "If you confess with your mouth the Lord Jesus and believe in your heart that God has raised Him from the dead, you will be saved. For with the heart one believes unto righteousness, and with the mouth confession is made unto salvation" (Rom. 10:9-10, NKJV).

We trust that you are now ready to pray with us. From your heart, express the following prayer to God who wants so much for you to have an intimate, personal relationship with Him:

Heavenly Father, thank you for showing me that I am a sinner in need of a Savior. Thank you for sending Jesus to be my Savior.

I have sinned against you in so many ways, dear God. I humbly confess my sins to you now. I believe that Jesus died for my sins. I now receive Jesus Christ as my personal Savior and Lord. I believe that you, Father God, have raised Him from the dead. Thank you, mighty God, for bringing my spirit to life by your Holy Spirit who is within me. Thank you, Lord Jesus, for being willing to take my place and to pay the price for my sins by dying on the cross and shedding your precious blood for me. I rejoice in the fact that

I will never be the same as I was before I prayed this prayer. I have been born again. I am a new creation in Christ. In Jesus' name I pray. Amen.

Now you are ready to read the chapters of this book with spiritual understanding, because you are a child of God, a member of God's family. Your name is now written in the Lamb's Book of Life, and you are assured of eternal and abundant life with God. Your new life has already begun, right here, right now. God loves you with an everlasting, unconditional love, and He wants you to know Him intimately, in all His fullness and glory.

May this book help you to grow in Christ, and in your knowledge of God.

PART I

WHO GOD IS

PART I

WHO GOD IS

Hear, O Israel:
The Lord our God is one Lord.
(Deut. 6:4)

When God appeared to Moses in the burning bush, He told him, "Unto thee it was shown, that thou mightest know that the Lord he is God; there is none else beside him" (Deut. 4:35). Both Judaism and Christianity are, therefore, monotheistic (holding to a belief in only one God), and this one, true God is our heavenly Father, the Creator of the universe and the Sustainer of all life.

Even though the Lord our God is one God, in the essence of His being, He is three distinct persons – the Father, the Son, and the Holy Spirit. The Church refers to these three as the Trinity.

The special significance of each member of the Trinity is discussed thoroughly in the first three chapters of *Knowing God Intimately*. Likewise, each is referred to frequently throughout the book.

To know that God is three persons in One is vitally important to the believer. Our God is one God, eternally existent in three persons. It was He who gave the Ten Commandments to Moses on Mount Sinai, and the first of these commandments is: "Thou shalt have none other gods before me" (Deut. 5:11). This first commandment establishes for all believers the truth that to worship anyone or anything other than God is the biggest mistake a person can make.

In fact, to put anyone or anything before Him leads a person into various forms of sin, as Paul points out, "For this reason God gave them up to vile passions" (Rom. 1:26, NKJV).

Sometimes, for example, our job or career may come between us and God. This happens when we forget to trust God to meet our needs, and consequently, we shut Him out of our lives, thinking erroneously that we can meet our own needs in our way and timing. Throughout *Knowing God Intimately* you will see how God desires to provide for us beyond all that we can ask or think when we become totally dependent on Him. He is willing and able to meet every need we have.

The story is told of a little girl who was sick in bed. Over the head of her bed hung the portrait of Jesus painted by Warner

Sallman. On the opposite wall, there was a mirror. As the child lay in bed, looking at the mirror, she could see the picture of Jesus, and this brought great hope and comfort to her. One day, however, as she was beginning to feel better, her mother discovered the little girl sitting up in bed and crying.

"Darling, why are you crying?" her mother asked.

"Mommy, every time I see myself I can't see Jesus," the little girl exclaimed.

She had learned a very important lesson. Just as soon as she was feeling better and sitting up in bed, her own reflection in the mirror had replaced the reflection of Jesus which earlier had brought her so much peace and comfort. It is true that as soon as we put the focus on ourselves we can no longer see God.

As you continue your reading of *Knowing God Intimately*, it is our deepest desire that you will come to know Him so well and fall in love with Him so deeply that you will want to serve Him only and give Him first place in your life at all times.

1

KNOWING GOD, THE FATHER

No man knoweth the Son, but the Father;
neither knoweth any man the Father,
save the Son, and he to whomsoever
the Son will reveal him.
(Matt. 11:27)

Abba, Father

The Apostle Paul wrote, "For as many as are led by the Spirit of God, these are the sons of God. For you did not receive the spirit of bondage again to fear, but you received the Spirit of adoption by whom we cry out, 'Abba, Father.' The Spirit Himself bears witness with our spirit that we are children of God" (Rom. 8:14-16, NKJV).

As we have already pointed out, God is three persons – the Father, the Son, and the Holy Spirit. He wants us to know Him as our Father. Indeed, He wants us to know Him as "Abba, Father." The word *abba* is an Aramaic term used to address one's father in a very familiar, loving way. It comes close to meaning the same thing as "daddy" or "papa."

Many people have a hard time thinking of God in these familiar terms, because they see

Him as the august, sober Ruler of the universe. Or they may feel intimidated by His glorious majesty, pristine holiness, awesome power, perfect goodness, or uncompromising justice. How we perceive God determines the kind of relationship we will have with Him.

Truly, He is our King, and His greatness far surpasses that of any earthly king. In fact, we can scarcely comprehend the greatness of our God. Nonetheless, He is our Father – Abba, Father – our "papa." When we see Him as our "papa," we can draw very close to Him, for everyone desires a close relationship with a loving father. He desires that we know Him not only as our Creator, but also affectionately as our Abba, Father.

Yes, God is our King, and we are His subjects, but it is likewise true that He is our Father who protects us, provides for us, and blesses us, because we are His greatly loved children. Certainly it is possible to be devoted to a king or a leader, and to serve such a ruler with loyalty and reverence. As children of our heavenly Father, however, we are able to go beyond loyalty and reverence, into a warm and wonderful intimacy with our Father.

"The fear of the Lord is the beginning of knowledge" (Prov. 1:7), but note that this is only the beginning of our relationship with

God. "Fear," in this context, means reverential awe and respect. An awed, hushed respect for God is the natural response of sinful people to a perfect God, but it is possible for each of us to go beyond this level in our relationship with God, because He wants us to know Him intimately, out of love, without any fear. Indeed, His perfect love casts out all fear. (See 1 John 4:17.)

It is the Father's overwhelming love for us that enables us to enter into a deeply personal relationship with Him. A realization of His love leads us into the place of fellowship with Him that He always wanted for us. Because He loves us so much we are able to "climb up into His lap," and find and receive His nurturance like little children in the lap of a loving papa.

As we find this place in God we are able to become as little children are – trusting, loving, obedient, open, honest, vulnerable, joyful, tender, teachable, and hopeful. God responds to our desire to have a close relationship with Him by taking delight in us like a father would take delight in his child. We then discover that we truly are the apple of His eye.

God longs to have such a relationship with you. This is why He created you in the first place. In the following pages you will be able to search through His Word and discover that God truly is your Father, and you will get to know your "papa God" so much better.

A Letter From the Father to You

You are My child,[1] and I am your Father.[2] I love you with an everlasting love.[3] Remember this, nothing in all the world will ever be able to separate you from the love I have for you.[4] I have set My love upon you and I have chosen you, because I love you.[5] Enjoy My lovingkindness, dear child.[6]

I promise never to take My kindness away from you.[7] My love for you is greater than you can possibly imagine. In fact, I gave My only begotten Son so that, through believing in Him, you would never perish, but have everlasting life.[8] I gave Jesus to be the sacrifice for your sins.[9] I ask only that you believe in Him,[10] receive Him,[11] and then you will be able to abide in His love.[12]

One of My commandments is that you should love others in the same way I love you and Jesus loves you.[13] This will give you happiness, My child.[14] It pleases Me when you love Me with all your heart and understanding.[15] This means more to Me than any offering or sacrifice ever could.[16]

I draw you to myself with the great lovingkindness that I hold for you.[17] Remember, when you draw near to Me, I will draw near to you,[18] and I will always take great delight in such intimacy with you.[19] My child, you are the apple of My eye.[20] My banner of love flies over you at all times.[21] You truly are My beloved.[22] I have always loved you.[23]

My love for you will always be patient, and it will never fail.[24] My precious child, always let My love for you remove all fear from your life.[25] I will be certain to make all things work together for your good.[26] Your eyes have not seen, and your ears have not heard all the things that I've prepared for you.[27] Therefore, My loved one, I ask you to keep yourself in My love,[28] and let your heart cry unto Me, "Abba Father."[29]

References: (1) John 1:12; (2) Mark 14:36; (3) Jeremiah 31:3; (4) Romans 8:38-39; (5) Psalms 91:14; (6) Psalms 25:6; (7) Isaiah 54:10; (8) John 3:16; (9) Galatians 2:20; (10) John 11:25; (11) John 1:12; (12) John 15:10; (13) John 14:21; (14) Psalms 144:15; (15) Mark 12:30-33; (16) Mark 12:33; (17) Jeremiah 31:3; (18) James 4:8; (19) John 14:21; (20) Deuteronomy 32:10; (21) Song of Solomon 2:4; (22) Song of Solomon 6:3; (23) Malachi 1:2; (24) 1 Corinthians 13:4; (25) 1 John 4:18; (26) Romans 8:28; (27) 1 Corinthians 2:9; (28) Jude 21; (29) Romans 8:15.

A Father's Heart

In his *Dictionary of the English Language*, written in 1775, Samuel Johnson gives us a good picture of what it means to be a father by defining three words that are related to this important role. The first is "papa," which Johnson defines as "A fond name for father, used in many languages." The second is "fatherly," the adverb which means, "Paternal; like a father; tender; protecting; careful." The third is "fatherliness," which this early dictionary defines as being, "The tenderness of a father; paternal kindness."

Our God is a Father who embodies all of these qualities. He is our tender, protecting, kind, and caring heavenly "Papa," who always wants the best for us. His love touches us, redeems us, heals us, supports us, keeps us, helps us, guides us, corrects us, and blesses us. In fact, His love surrounds us at all times.

Our Father's love for us surpasses the love of human fathers. A lady whose father had died more than twenty years before was reminiscing about him to a group of other women. She said that she could still remember her father's warm embrace at a desperate time in her life when she was seventeen. Her boyfriend had broken her heart by leaving her for another classmate.

It was the hardest thing she'd ever experienced. She hid herself in her bedroom and began to sob with her head buried in her pillow. In a few moments, she heard her father's footsteps in the hallway. Without saying a word, he came into her room and sat on the edge of her bed. Caringly, he lifted his daughter into his arms, and simply held her. She said, "I can still feel his arms around me, holding me close, keeping me safe. Even though I miss my father, I can still feel the warmth of his embrace."

This was a healing moment in her life. Her father's love helped her to be restored to wholeness. It is the same with our Father in heaven. He is our safe place at all times. He is always there, our tender, caring, supportive, "Papa," who knows all about us, and loves us to wholeness.

The heart of our Father in heaven is always open toward us. He knows what we need, and He is always at work to meet our needs.

Jesus Reveals the Father to Us

God is our Father. When we fully comprehend this fact, everything in our lives takes on new meaning. As our Father, God takes good care of us. He loves us. He protects us, and defends us. He watches out for us. He meets our every need. He wants to spend time with us. He takes delight in us. He wants to teach us everything that He knows will benefit us. He guides us. He holds our hand. He lifts us up.

We are children in His royal family. This means that we are princes and princesses in the household of God. As such, we are entitled to all the privileges and blessings of the King.

We are joint-heirs with Jesus of all the royal blessings bestowed by Father God upon His children. Because we have been adopted into His family, we are able to claim the inheritance that God has provided for us. Paul wrote, "For as many as are led by the Spirit of God, these are sons of God. . . .The Spirit Himself bears witness with our spirit that we are children of God, and if children, then heirs – heirs of God and joint heirs with Christ" (Rom. 8:14-17, NKJV).

That we are permitted to call God our Father is a thrilling realization. In fact, this is one important hallmark of Christianity – we see God as our own Father. By way of contrast, Muslims have ninety-nine names for God, but not one of them is close to "our Father."

God is our Father, but He is never a grandfather, because God has no grandchildren. We must either know Him personally, first-hand, or we will not know Him at all.

Made in the Image of Our Father

The Bible tells us that we are made in God's own image. (See Gen. 1:26-27.) David Hartman, a television journalist and actor, credits his father, a Methodist minister, with helping him to get through several major challenges of his life. His dad used to say, "Remember this, David: you're made in God's image, and so you have His power in you. Who's going to waste that kind of power?"

Those words helped the young man through many difficult circumstances, including the time when he was dropped from pre-flight training with the U.S. Air Force because he was too tall. (David had always dreamed of being a jet pilot with the U.S. Air Force.) Another time he remembered his father's words was when he was trying to find an acting job in New York City. He got off the bus, thinking that he would never be able to get through to the key decision-makers. Instead of giving in to the negativity, however, he asked himself what his father would do in a similar situation. His confidence renewed as he dropped a dime into the pay phone. He got through to the director immediately, and his first appointment for show business was secured!

The knowledge that we are created in God's own image does give us a sense of confidence and assurance that we would never know otherwise. David remembered his father's wise and comforting words as he faced the challenges of his life. As children of our Father in heaven, it would always be best for us to remember God's words to us, to know that we are created in the image of our Father, to experience His power at work in us, and to make choices that we know He would want for us.

Our Father believes in us, and He always wants the very best for us!

God First

Jesus has a close and intimate relationship with His Father, and He wants us to have the same kind of fellowship with Him and our Father in heaven. Jesus uses the word "Father" to address God more than 200 times in the gospels. When He prays, He prays to His Father. When He preaches, He points us to the Father. When He ministers to the needs of people, He praises the Father. Clearly, He wants us to know the Father.

Oswald Chambers writes, "Begin to know Him now, and finish never." The one thing that is most important in all of life is knowing God, because knowing God is the one thing that will go on forever. Jesus said, "But seek first the kingdom of God and His righteousness, and all these things shall be added to you" (Matt. 6:33, NKJV). First things first. The highest priority is knowing God, and His righteousness.

The way of Christ is the way into the very heart of God. St. Augustine prayed, "O Thou who art the Light of the minds that know Thee, the Life of the souls that love Thee, and the Strength of the wills that serve Thee; help us so to know Thee that we may truly love Thee; so to love Thee that we may fully serve Thee, whom to serve is perfect freedom."

We respond to the Father's great love for us by putting Him first in our lives. Jesus said, "For the Father Himself loves you, because you have loved Me, and have believed that I came forth from God" (John 16:27, NKJV).

Jesus' Intercessory Prayer for Us

Just prior to His arrest and crucifixion, Jesus prayed, "Father, the hour has come. Glorify Your Son, that Your Son also may glorify You. . . .And this is eternal life, that they may know You, the only true God, and Jesus Christ whom You have sent" (John 17:1-3, NKJV). One of Jesus' final requests to the Father in our behalf is that we would know the Father.

In this exciting prayer of intercession, which is still being fulfilled in the world, Jesus prays for us, asking the Father, ". . .that they all may be one, as You, Father, are in Me, and I in You; that they also may be one in Us, that the world may believe that You sent Me" (John 17:21, NKJV).

When we are truly one with the Father and His Son, our Savior and Lord Jesus Christ, the world will finally understand that God sent Jesus. This is an important reason why we must get to know God as our Father, as Jesus knows Him. The Father is in Jesus, and Jesus is in the Father. We are to be one with them and in them. This implies ultimate relationship and personal intimacy. It also reminds us that, as Christians, we are bearers of the name of Christ, with a responsibility to bring honor and glory to that name at all times.

Jesus reveals the Father's glory to us: "And the glory which You gave Me I have given them, that they may be one just as We are one; I in them, and You in Me; that they may be made perfect in one, and that the world may know that You have sent Me, and have loved them as You have loved Me" (John 17:22-23, NKJV).

The unity Jesus wants us to have with one another will stem directly from our unity with Him and the Father. As we exhibit such love and unity, the world will truly know that God sent Jesus because He loves them.

Jesus concludes this prayer with a note of hope and victory: "O righteous Father! The world has not known You, but I have known You; and these [His disciples] have known that You sent Me. And I have declared to them Your name, and will declare it, that the love with which You loved Me may be in them, and I in them" (John 17:25-26, NKJV). What a prayer Jesus prayed for us, that the same love with which the Father loved Jesus would be in us.

Our minds find this difficult to grasp. No wonder, for this love cannot be grasped by our mind. No, it is revealed to our hearts by the Holy Spirit. As we meditate on this prayer of Jesus, our own spirit seems to enlarge with joy. His word comes alive within us and we sense God's love for us. We are His children and He fills us with His love. He fills us with himself.

The Father's Personality

Jesus has declared the name of God to us. In His names, we learn so much about our heavenly Father. Our God is a living personality; He has a will, emotions, and intelligence. The Bible (the Father's love letter to His children) helps us to understand the personality of our Father:

God is alive. "The Lord liveth" (2 Sam. 22:47).

God loves; in fact, He is love. "He who does not love does not know God, for God is love" (1 John 4:8, NKJV).

God is patient. "One day is with the Lord as a thousand years, and a thousand years as one day" (2 Pet. 3:8).

God is kind. "But You are God, ready to pardon, gracious and merciful, slow to anger, abundant in kindness, and did not forsake them" (Neh. 9:17, NKJV).

God is merciful. "Thou, O Lord, art a God full of compassion, and gracious, longsuffering, and plenteous in mercy and truth" (Ps. 86:15).

God is forgiving. "Thou art a God ready to pardon" (Neh. 9:17).

God is supportive. "He will not fail thee, nor forsake thee" (Deut. 31:6).

God is righteous. "The Lord is righteous" (2 Chron. 12:6).

God is slow to anger. "He is gracious and merciful, slow to anger, and of great kindness" (Joel 2:13).

God grieves. "And the Lord . . . was grieved in His heart" (Gen. 6:6, NKJV).

God experiences jealousy. "You shall not go after other gods, the gods of the peoples who are all around you (for the Lord your God is a jealous God among you), lest the anger of the Lord your God be aroused against you and destroy you from the face of the earth" (Deut. 6:14-15, NKJV).

God loves His children. "So I have looked for You in the sanctuary, to see Your power and Your glory. Because Your lovingkindness is better than life, my lips shall praise You. Thus I will bless You while I live; I will lift up my hands in Your name" (Ps. 63:3-4, NKJV).

God experiences joy. "Do not sorrow, for the joy of the Lord is your strength" (Neh. 8:10, NKJV).

God does not change. "I am the Lord, I change not" (Mal. 3:6).

All of these attributes of the divine personality show us that our Father is a Person with whom we can have an intimate, personal relationship. He is not some cold and distant deity. He experiences the full range of emotions; therefore, He understands us completely, and He wants us to understand Him as well.

Because He knows our feelings and weaknesses, He is able to have compassion upon us in our weakness. Perhaps the best picture of God is painted in the book of Galatians where Paul outlines the fruit of the Spirit. These are the essential qualities and characteristics of our Father: "But the fruit of the Spirit is love, joy, peace, longsuffering, kindness, goodness, faithfulness, gentleness, self-control. Against such there is not law" (Gal. 5:22-23, NKJV).

Children of God

We are not the natural-born children of God. He has only one begotten Son (Jesus), but when we are born again, we are adopted into His family through the blood of Jesus. The Holy Spirit assures us that we are now members of the family of God. We are His children, His heirs, and joint-heirs with Christ.

God is our Father, and we are brothers and sisters of Jesus. The Father has bequeathed His kingdom, and all its blessings to us. Paul writes, "Blessed be the God and Father of our Lord Jesus Christ, who has blessed us with every spiritual blessing in the heavenly places in Christ, just as He chose us in Him before the foundation of the world, that we should be holy and without blame before Him in love" (Eph. 1:3-4, NKJV).

A young woman who is now a devoted Christian spent the first thirty years of her life searching for her "father." Her earthly dad had died of a massive coronary when she was only eight years old. Her search for a "surrogate father" led her down some dark avenues of promiscuity, depression, and addiction, until one day a young man came to her with some good news. He told her that God was her heavenly Father who loved her so much that He had sent Jesus to be her Savior.

She said, "It was as if an explosion took place deep within me. I realized then and there that the father I had been searching for all my life was God! His great love for me drew me close to Him, and I literally ran into His arms. I've never been the same since the day I found my Father." Many others have testified to the same experience.

The longing of the human soul is fulfilled and satisfied only in knowing God. All of us are involved in this quest, even though some may not realize it. It is a quest to know God as our loving Father.

John Piper writes, "To be satisfied in God is the essence of what it means to love God. Loving God may include obeying all His commands; it may include believing all His Word; it may include thanking Him for all His gifts; but the essence of loving God is enjoying all He is. It is this enjoyment of God that glorifies His worth most fully, especially when all around our soul gives way."

Now hope does not disappoint, because the love of God has been poured out in our hearts by the Holy Spirit who was given to us.
(Rom. 5:5, NKJV)

Prayer of Response: Dear God, you are my Abba-Father. Thank you for saving me and adopting me into your family. Knowing you as my Father gives me a deep sense of confidence, peace, joy, and love. As your child, I always want to put you first, and to please you in everything I say, think, and do. Thank you for fulfilling the longing of my heart. I love you, Father. In Jesus' name I pray, Amen.

2
KNOWING GOD, THE SON

Then Jesus cried out and said,
"He who believes in Me, believes not in Me
but in Him who sent Me.
And he who sees Me sees Him who sent Me."
(John 12:44-45, NKJV)

Knowing God Through Jesus

The Father sent Jesus, His only begotten Son, into the world, to pay the price for our sin and to deliver us from death and hell, and also to show us who God, the Father, is. In Jesus, we find our Father manifested in flesh and blood. The life of Jesus points us to God, the Father, and He has accomplished this through His life, death, burial, resurrection, and ascension.

The true purpose for which Jesus came to earth is summed up in the following passage, "To wit, that God was in Christ, reconciling the world unto himself, not imputing their trespasses unto them. . ." (2 Cor. 5:19). A sacrifice for all of our sins was required, and this sacrifice was something that human beings could not come up with on their own.

They needed a Savior who would break the chains of sin which had been forged by

Adam's disobedience in the Garden of Eden. Through the sacrifice of Jesus on the cross, those who believe in Him are able to return to the original position for which mankind was created – to have fellowship with the Father. It took a Man who was perfect – Jesus Christ, the Lord – to make that ultimate sacrifice for us.

Pause for a moment and consider the full extent of that sacrifice. Jesus, who was perfect in every respect and knew no sin, paid for our salvation through being betrayed, tortured, persecuted, and suffering a cruel and shameful death. His Father gave Him up for that purpose.

Jesus said, "I am the way, the truth, and the life: no man cometh unto the Father, but by me" (John 14:6). There is no other way than through Jesus to get to the Father.

God not only provided a way of redemption for us, but He revealed himself to us through Jesus so that we could understand Him and apprehend Him with our soul and spirit. As we walk with Jesus through the gospels, and listen to the first-hand accounts of those who knew Him intimately, we are drawn to God as our loving heavenly Father.

A Letter From the Father to You

Jesus is My beloved Son in whom I am well pleased.[1] I sent Him into the world so that whoever believes in Him would never perish, but have everlasting life.² Jesus has the power to forgive your sins.³ Therefore, I ask you to proclaim Him before other people so that He will be able to confess you before Me.⁴

My Son came to earth in order to seek and to save all who are lost.⁵ He has been with Me since the beginning.⁶ Without Him nothing was created.⁷ In Him you have found life, and you have discovered that His life is your light.⁸

Through knowing Jesus, you get to know Me.⁹ He is the light of the world.¹⁰ He is the door.¹¹ He is the way, the truth, and the life.¹²

Whatever you ask for in the name of Jesus, I will do for you.¹³ Through Jesus, you have peace with Me.¹⁴

You are complete in Him,¹⁵ for He is all, and in all.¹⁶ Let His words find their dwelling place within you.¹⁷

Let Jesus be your Lord at all times.¹⁸ Let Him have the preeminence in all that you say and do.¹⁹

References: (1) Matthew 3:17; (2) John 3:16; (3) Matthew 9:6; (4) Matthew 10:32-33; (5) Luke 19:10; (6) John 1:1-2; (7) John 1:3; (8) John 1:4; (9) John 8:19; (10) John 9:5; (11) John 10:9; (12) John 14:6;(13) John 16:23; (14) Romans 5:1; (15) Colossians 2:10; (16) Colossians 3:11; (17) Colossians 3:16; (18) John 9:38; (19) Colossians 1:18.

Jesus Reveals the Father to Us

Jesus is the Son of God. As such, He not only resembles His Father, but He actually is one with His Father. Philip asked Jesus to show him the Father, and Jesus responded, "Have I been with you so long, and yet you have not known Me, Philip? He who has seen Me has seen the Father; so how can you say, 'Show us the Father'? Do you not believe that I am in the Father, and the Father in Me? The words that I speak to you I do not speak on My own authority; but the Father who dwells in Me does the works. Believe Me that I am in the Father and the Father in Me" (John 14:9-11, NKJV).

To know Jesus better, we need to understand who He is and how the Father is manifested in and through Him:

Jesus is: ". . .the Christ, the Son of the living God" (Matt. 16:16).

Jesus is: "A Saviour, which is Christ the Lord" (Luke 2:11).

Jesus is: "The Lamb of God" (John 1:29).

Jesus is: "The Son of God" (John 1:34).

Jesus is: "The Messiah" (John 1:41).

Jesus is: "The son of man" (John 1:51).

Jesus is: "The bread of life" (John 6:35).

Jesus is: ". . .the light of the world" (John 8:12).

Jesus is: ". . .the door" (John 10:9).

Jesus is: "The good shepherd" (John 10:11).

Jesus is: ". . .the way, the truth, and the life" (John 14:6).

Jesus is: ". . .the true vine" (John 15:1).

Jesus is: ". . .the King of the Jews" (John 19:19).

Jesus is: "The Holy One and the Just" (Acts 3:14).

Jesus is: "The Deliverer" (Rom. 11:26).

Jesus is: "The author and finisher of our faith" (Heb. 12:2).

Jesus is: "The true light" (1 John 2:8).

Jesus is: "The faithful witness" (Rev. 1:5).

Jesus is: "The morning star" (Rev. 2:28).

Jesus is: "The Word of God" (Rev. 19:13).

Jesus is: "King of kings, and Lord of lords" (Rev. 19:16).

Jesus is: ". . .Alpha and Omega, the beginning and the end, the first and the last" (Rev. 22:13).

To know God through Jesus, therefore, is to know Him as the living God, the bread of life, the light of the world, the door, the Good

Shepherd, the Holy One, the Judge, the Deliverer, and everything else that Jesus represents to us, for He truly is everything to us.

Jesus Loves Me

Karl Barth, a German-Swiss theologian of the early twentieth century who wrote many books about God and the Bible, was asked (on the occasion of his eightieth birthday), "In all your years of studying about God and the Bible, what is the most important thing you've learned?"

The scholar paused pensively for a moment, and then stated simply, "I think it is this – 'Jesus loves me, this I know, for the Bible tells me so.'"

The theologian was referring to a song he had learned in Sunday school so many years before. It is indeed an important truth for all of us to remember, for Jesus' love is unconditional, and it is the most liberating force we can ever experience.

Many may know the song, "Jesus Loves Me," but some may not know its second verse: "Jesus loves me when I'm good, when I do the things I should. Jesus loves me when I'm bad, but it makes Him oh, so sad." It is true that Jesus' love is always in operation in our lives. He always loves us, but when we sin it brings grief to Him.

Let us never forget these words of our Savior Jesus Christ: "Verily, verily, I say unto you, he that heareth my word, and believeth on him that sent me, hath everlasting life, and shall not come into condemnation; but is passed from death unto life" (John 5:24).

A little poem by Annie Johnson Flint gives us a vivid insight into the love of God as it is so lavishly displayed to us through Jesus:

> God hath not promised skies always blue,
> Flower-strewn pathways all our lives through.
>
> God hath not promised sun without rain,
> Joy without sorrow, peace without pain.
>
> But God hath promised strength for the day,
> Rest for the laborer; light on the way.
>
> Grace for the trial, help from above,
> Unfailing sympathy – undying love.

Jesus Is Our Righteousness

Our God is righteous, and Jesus is our righteousness. "For he hath made him to be sin for us, who knew no sin; that we might be made the righteousness of God in him" (2 Cor. 5:21).

Paul put it this way also: "But of him are ye in Christ Jesus, who of God is made unto us wisdom, and righteousness, and sanctification, and redemption" (1 Cor. 1:30).

Knowing God through Jesus is receiving His righteousness. "And be found in him, not having mine own righteousness, which is of the law, but that which is through the faith of Christ, the righteousness which is of God by faith" (Phil. 3:9).

God's righteousness, as it has been revealed to us through Jesus, is just one aspect of His holiness. James Montgomery Boice explains it this way: "When we ask, 'What is right? What is moral?' we answer not by appealing to some independent moral standard, as if there could be a standard for anything apart from God, but rather by appealing to the will and nature of God Himself. The right is what God is and reveals to us."

Jesus Is Our Friend

Just as Abraham was called "the friend of God" (See James 2:23.), Jesus calls us His friends: "You are My friends if you do whatever I command you. No longer do I call you servants, for a servant does not know what his master is doing; but I have called you friends, for all things that I heard from

My Father I have made known to you. You did not choose Me, but I chose you and appointed you that you should go and bear fruit, and that your fruit should remain, that whatever you ask the Father in My name He may give you" (John 15:14-16, NKJV).

Our friendship with Jesus teaches us many things. One of the most important things it teaches us is how much the Father values our obedience to Him. If we are obedient, the Holy Spirit will reveal to us all that Jesus and the Father desire for us to know. In this way we get to know God in all His fullness, and God promises to answer our prayers. Because we obey Him, we are His friends. Though it amazes us to say it, we are the friends of God.

Jesus said, "He that hath my commandments, and keepeth them, he it is that loveth me: and he that loveth me shall be loved of my Father, and I will love him, and will manifest myself to him" (John 14:21). Jesus loves us and wants to manifest His love, power, and His presence to us and in us.

Jesus Is Our High Priest

Paul wrote, "For there is one God and one Mediator between God and men, the Man Christ Jesus" (1 Tim. 2:5, NKJV). Jesus leads us to the Father, reveals the Father to us, and opens up the Father's heart to us. The things Jesus did during His earthly ministry, likewise, reveal a great deal to us about the heart of our heavenly Father.

Jesus healed the sick, raised the dead, performed numerous miracles, challenged the hypocrites, preached God's Word, set the captives free, and sacrificed His own life for us. What do these things teach us about God? From Jesus' example, and His mediation for us, we see that God is just, compassionate, loving, powerful, and generous.

Jesus is now at God's right hand in heaven, ever living to pray and make intercession for us. (See Rom. 8:34.) Jesus is our great High Priest. He is touched by the feeling of our infirmities, and He beckons us to come boldly to the throne of God's grace that we may obtain mercy and find grace to help us in our times of need. (See Heb. 4:14-16.)

The Touch of the Master's Hand

Jesus' disciples frequently called Him "Master," because a master is a teacher of the highest quality. He is our Master as well, and from Him we learn so much.

Wishing to encourage her young son's progress on the piano, a mother took her boy to a Paderewski concert. After they were seated, the mother spotted a friend in the audience, and she walked down the aisle to greet her. While she was gone, the lad seized the opportunity to explore the great concert hall. Somehow he managed to find his way through a door that was marked, "No admittance."

When the house lights dimmed, the mother returned to her seat only to discover that her son was not where she had left him. His seat was empty, and she was filled with a sense of panic! Not knowing where to turn in the darkness, she stood frozenly as the curtains parted and all eyes in the auditorium turned toward the impressive Steinway on stage. In horror, the mother saw her son seated at the keyboard! She heard him innocently picking out the bars of "Twinkle, Twinkle, Little Star."

Just then, Paderewski, the great piano master, made his grand entrance. He quickly moved to the piano and whispered to the little boy, "Don't quit. Keep on playing." Then, the great pianist leaned over, reached down with his left hand and began filling the bass part. Soon his right arm reached around the boy and the maestro began to add a running obligato to the tune.

Paderewski truly was a master of his art, for he had transformed this awkward, embarrassing moment into a wonderfully creative experience for all concerned. The audience, including the boy's mother, was mesmerized by this opening performance.

The same thing happens when we allow God, through Jesus, to help us in any given situation of our lives. It is then that we discover that the touch of the Master's hand makes all the difference in the world. At such times we sense the Master's loving arms enveloping us, and our confidence is renewed.

There is a dynamic poem which shares this same truth with us. It is entitled "The Touch of the Master's Hand." This ballad tells the story of an old violin that was being auctioned off. When the auctioneer first showed the dusty, scratchy instrument to the crowd, the opening bids were quite small. Then, however, a man came up to the platform and asked the auctioneer if he would let him play the violin. The auctioneer agreed, and bids were suspended momentarily.

The man exhibited his skill as a master violinist, and his touch changed the worth of the violin in the audience's eyes. After his performance, the auctioneer lifted the violin with its bow for all to see, and then he proceeded with the bidding. The musician's performance had totally changed the situation. The worth of the violin had increased a thousandfold!

The poem concludes with these words:

> And many a man with life out of tune,
> And battered and scarred with sin,
> Is auctioned cheap to the thoughtless crowd,
> Much like the old violin.

> But the Master comes, and the foolish crowd
> Never can quite understand,
> The worth of a soul, and the change that's wrought,
> By the touch of the Master's hand.

The touch of the Master's hand transforms our lives, and His touch can totally change any situation we face. It is only the Master's touch that is able to change despair into hope; death into life; grief into joy; sickness into health; depression into gladness; fear into love; worry into peace; weakness into strength; darkness into life; coldness into warmth; and defeat into victory.

Jesus is the Master who broke the bonds of death for all of us. He took our sins upon himself, and set us totally free. He brought light into the darkness, and gave the world new hope. "For as by one man's [Adam's] disobedience many were made sinners, so also by one Man's [Jesus'] obedience many will be made righteous. . . .so that as sin reigned in death, even so grace might reign through righteousness to eternal life through Jesus Christ our Lord" (Rom. 5:19-21, NKJV).

Jesus Teaches Us About the Father

We learn much about God from Jesus' example, and we also learn a great deal about the Father from Jesus' words. As we listen to Jesus, He reveals to us that the Father is:

Our true Father. "Call no man your father upon the earth: for one is your Father, which is in heaven" (Matt. 23:9).

True. "God is true" (John 3:33).

Spirit. "God is Spirit, and those who worship Him must worship in spirit and truth" (John 4:24, NKJV).

The vinedresser. "I am the true vine, and My Father is the vinedresser" (John 15:1, NKJV).

The Giver of good gifts. "If you then, being evil, know how to give good gifts to your children, how much more will your Father who is in heaven give good things to those who ask Him!" (Matt. 7:11, NKJV).

Forgiving. "And whenever you stand praying, if you have anything against anyone, forgive him, that your Father in heaven may also forgive you your trespasses" (Mark 11:25, NKJV).

All-powerful. "Abba, Father, all things are possible for You" (Mark 14:36, NKJV).

All-knowing. "You are those who justify yourselves before men, but God knows your hearts. For what is highly esteemed among men is an abomination in the sight of God" (Luke 16:15, NKJV).

From Jesus, therefore, we learn a great deal about God, our Father. In Jesus, we see God in the flesh. One of the names of Jesus, in fact, is Emmanuel, and this means "God with us." (See Matt. 1:23.) God manifests himself to us through His Son, Jesus Christ.

A wealthy man in his early sixties came to a major discovery during the year after his beloved wife died from an illness, and his daughter committed suicide as the result of an LSD trip. It was, understandably, the hardest year of his life. Though he had attended church most of his life, religion had never been a personal thing to him. His primary pursuits were the accumulation of wealth and property and travel. In fact, he had two or three homes, a condominium, and a yacht.

When he lost the two most important people in his life, however, he realized the emptiness and futility of those years of self-aggrandizement and materialism. He still had his homes and his yacht, but life no longer had any meaning for him.

In total desperation, he walked into a large cathedral, knelt in a pew, and began to ask God, "Why?" For the first time in years, pent-up tears were released and they streamed down his cheeks. Through the tears he noticed a crucifix above the altar, and He felt as if God was saying, "Jesus died for *you*." He was stunned by the personal tone of this thought, because He had never realized that Jesus had died for him. Somehow, he assumed that Jesus had died for the sins of the whole world, but for him personally?

The more he thought about it, the more he realized that this must be true. He got up from his seat, walked to the front of the church, and knelt at the altar. There he gave his heart to Jesus, and he promised his newfound Lord that from that point on he would give Him everything – his life, his money, his things.

Jesus heard his prayer, and saved him. From then on, until his death, this wealthy man spent his life serving God by helping others. Knowing Jesus had made everything new to him. He said, "It was trouble that brought me to Jesus, and now I've found a far richer purpose and calling in life than I ever could have known without Him."

A. W. Tozer wrote, "How are we going to know what God is like so that we may know whether we're like God? The answer is: God is like Christ, for Christ is God manifest to mankind. By looking at our Lord Jesus we will know what God is like and will know what we have to be like to experience the unbroken and continuous presence of God."

> *Blessed be the God and Father of our*
> *Lord Jesus Christ, who hath blessed*
> *us with all spiritual blessings in*
> *heavenly places in Christ.*
> (Eph. 1:3)

Prayer of Response: Dear Father, thank you for sending Jesus, your only begotten Son, to be both my Savior and Lord. I realize that He is everything to me, and I love Him with all my heart. With your help, I will walk in the footsteps of Jesus wherever I go, and I will give Him the preeminence in all that I say and do. In Jesus' name I pray, Amen.

3

KNOWING GOD, THE HOLY SPIRIT

But the Helper, the Holy Spirit, whom the Father will send in My name, He will teach you all things, and bring to your remembrance all things that I said to you.
(John 14:26, NKJV)

Knowing God as the Holy Spirit

The third person of the Trinity is the Holy Spirit. When it was no longer possible for Jesus to be with us in the flesh – after His redeeming work was done, and He could return to His glory with the Father in heaven – our loving God sent us a Helper and Comforter to take His place. The Father sent the Holy Spirit to indwell us so that we could be able to hear God's voice and be reminded of everything Jesus had taught us when He walked this earth.

In a very real sense, Jesus represents to fallen humanity the ability to walk and talk with God as Adam and Eve had been able to do in the Garden of Eden. Until they fell, they had been able to walk and talk with God openly and freely. That ceased as a result of their sin, and they became mortal human beings. The word "mortal" stems from a root which means "death," and it, therefore, means that all mortals are "subject to death."

Adam and Eve, as mortals, could no longer enjoy fellowship with the Father because their spirits had been tainted with death. Their sin had separated them from God. Jesus came to show mortal men and women that such fellowship with God is still possible, and He paved the way for this vital relationship with God to be restored.

After Jesus' work was finished, the Holy Spirit came so that we could, once again, walk and talk with God as He had planned for us to do from the very beginning. It is by faith that we are able to hear the Holy Spirit speaking to us. It is by faith that we are able to speak to the Father and know that He hears us. John records this promise from God: "And if we know that he hear us, whatsoever we ask, we know that we have the petitions that we desired of him" (1 John 5:15).

John also wrote the following: "Hereby know we that we dwell in him [God], and he in us, because he hath given us of his Spirit. And we have seen and do testify that the Father sent the Son to be the Saviour of the world. Whosoever shall confess that Jesus is the Son of God, God dwelleth in him, and he in God" (1 John 4:13-15).

This passage reveals several things about God to us. First, it is a clear statement that He does, indeed, exist in three persons – Father, Son, and Holy Spirit. Second, it shows us that God sent Jesus to be the Savior of the world. Third, the way that we know that we dwell in God and that God dwells in us is by His Holy Spirit whom He sent to us.

What a wonderful Scripture this is. As we read and think on it, God gives us the faith to believe that we really do dwell in God and He really does dwell in us. As we come to this realization, our lives are changed forever.

The Holy Spirit teaches us, comforts us, convicts us, reminds us of truth, prays for us, quickens our mortal bodies, guides us, teaches us, and speaks to us. He also empowers us for ministry and righteous living. Above all, however, He indwells us, always directing our focus back to the Father and to our Lord Jesus. He is God with us and in us. In the following sections of this chapter we will take an in-depth look, from the Scriptures (which were inspired by the Spirit of God), at all the wonderful blessings we have through the Holy Spirit, whom the Father so lovingly sent to us.

A Letter From the Father to You

Dearly beloved, I want you to remember that your body is the temple of My Holy Spirit.[1] Keep your hope in Me, because I have poured out My love, through the Holy Spirit, into your heart.[2]

My Holy Spirit will guide you into all truth. Remember that He will not be speaking of himself to you. Instead, He will speak My words to you, and He will even reveal future things to you.[3] I love to give My Holy Spirit to everyone who asks Me,[4] because He is your Helper,[5] Comforter,[6] and Teacher.[7] When My Holy Spirit comes upon you, you will receive power to be a witness for Jesus wherever you go.[8]

Be continuously filled with My Holy Spirit every day.[9] His infilling in your life will enable you to speak My Word with great boldness.[10]

My Holy Spirit brings help to your weaknesses in prayer when you do not know how to pray. My Holy Spirit will make intercession for you with groanings that cannot be uttered.[11]

The fruit of the Holy Spirit in your life is love, joy, peace, longsuffering, gentleness, goodness, faith, meekness, temperance, and there is no law against these things.

Therefore, live in My Holy Spirit, and walk in Him.[12]

It is the Holy Spirit who bears witness with your spirit that you are My child. As one of My children, you are one of My heirs, and you are a joint-heir with Jesus.[13] I want you to have the inheritance I've kept for you.[14] When the enemy tries to come into your life like a flood, just remember that My Holy Spirit will raise up a standard against him in your behalf.[15]

My Holy Spirit will change you from glory to glory and make you more like Jesus.[16] He will teach you what you should say in every given situation.[17] He will enable you to speak My Word with great boldness.[18] Let My Holy Spirit guide you at all times.[19]

References: (1) 1 Corinthians 6:19; (2) Romans 5:5; (3) John 16:13; (4) Luke 11:13; (5) John 16:7; (6) John 14:16; (7) John 16:13; (8) Acts 1:8; (9) Ephesians 5:18; (10) Acts 4:31; (11) Romans 8:26; (12) Galatians 5:22-25; (13) Romans 8:16-18; (14) Ephesians 1:11; (15) Isaiah 59:19; (16) 2 Corinthians 3:18; (17) Luke 12:12; (18) Acts 4:31-33; (19) Romans 8:14.

The Holy Spirit Is the Spirit of Truth

The Holy Spirit is the Spirit of Truth. As we get to know Him, we discover the truth of God. He inspired the Word of Truth, and the Father sent Him to us in order to guide us into all truth. The Holy Spirit possesses the truth, reveals the truth, confers the truth, leads us into the truth, testifies to the truth, and defends the truth.

The Scriptures assign various names to the Holy Spirit, and each of these gives us insights into the very nature and personality of our God. He is:

> *The Spirit of holiness. (See Rom. 1:4.)*
> *The Spirit of grace. (See Heb. 10:29.)*
> *The Spirit of truth. (See 1 John 5:6-8.)*
> *The Spirit of life. (See Rom. 8:2.)*
> *The Spirit of wisdom and understanding.*
>   *(See Isa. 11:2.)*
> *The Spirit of counsel and might. (See Isa. 11:2.)*
> *The Spirit of knowledge and of the fear of the*
>   *Lord. (See Isa. 11:2.)*
> *The Spirit of promise. (See Eph. 1:13.)*
> *The Spirit of glory. (See 1 Pet. 4:14.)*
> *The Spirit of God. (See 1 Cor. 3:16.)*
> *The Spirit of Christ. (See Rom. 8:9.)*
> *The Spirit of adoption. (See Rom. 8:15-16.)*

The Holy Spirit works in our lives to help us to know God and His ways. Other responsibilities of the Holy Spirit include the following:

> *He leads us to salvation by convicting us of*
>   *our sins. (See John 16:8-11.)*
> *He testifies to us of Jesus Christ.*
>   *(See John 15:26.)*
> *He dwells within the believer. (See 1 Cor. 6:19.)*
> *He seals the believer. (See Eph. 1:13-14.)*

He infills the believer. (See Eph. 5:18.)
He empowers the believer. (See Acts 1:8.)
He guides the believer. (See Rom. 8:14.)
He anoints the believer. (See 1 John 2:27.)

The Holy Spirit is the Spirit of truth, and He leads us into all truth.

The Holy Spirit Is Our Teacher

One of the major works of the Holy Spirit in our lives is to teach us more about God, our Father. Paul discusses this at some length in his first letter to the Corinthians: "But as it is written, eye hath not seen, nor ear heard, neither have entered into the heart of man, the things which God hath prepared for them that love him. But God hath revealed them unto us by his Spirit: for the Spirit searcheth all things, yea, the deep things of God" (1 Cor. 2:9-10).

The Holy Spirit reveals the deep things of God to us. Paul continues with this thought in a subsequent verse: "Now we have received, not the spirit of the world, but the spirit which is of God; that we might know the things that are freely given to us of God" (1 Cor. 2:12).

The Holy Spirit knows the Father intimately, because the Holy Spirit is the third person of the Trinity (Father, Son, and Holy Spirit). What He knows He is willing to share with us, because He feels for us, understands us, and knows what we need.

One specific area in which the Holy Spirit helps us concerns prayer. "Likewise the Spirit also helps in our weaknesses. For we do not know what we should pray for as we ought, but the Spirit Himself makes intercession for us with groanings which cannot be uttered" (Rom. 8:26, NKJV). In fact, the Holy Spirit makes intercession for us according to the will of God. (See Rom. 8:27.)

As the Holy Spirit teaches us in all areas, we are taught of God, and we are taught about God.

The Holy Spirit Supplies Us With God's Power

Through the Holy Spirit's ministry we find power for living. It is supernatural power that affects everything it comes in contact with. For example, the Holy Spirit gives us dynamic power for witnessing: "But you shall receive power when the Holy Spirit has come upon you; and you shall be witnesses to Me in Jerusalem, and in all Judea and Samaria, and to the end of the earth" (Acts 1:8, NKJV).

He gives power to our words, and He makes the presence of God within us very real. To be filled with the Spirit, therefore, is to be filled with the power of God. Dr. Bill Bright, the founder of Campus Crusade for Christ, said: "If there were only one truth I could share with the Christian world, it would be 'how to be filled with the Holy Spirit,' for there is no single truth that is more important to the believer."

It is the Holy Spirit who leads us into a godly life. "For as many as are led by the Spirit of God, these are the sons of God" (Rom. 8:14, NKJV).

The Holy Spirit Brings God's Comfort to Us

Jesus said He would pray and ask the Father to send the Holy Spirit in our behalf. (See John 14:14-18.) He promised that this Comforter would abide with us forever. That's an exciting thought, and it's because this is true that we are able to experience the comforting presence of God in the circumstances of our lives.

Jesus explains this further: "But the Comforter, which is the Holy Ghost, whom the Father will send in my name, he shall teach you all things, and bring all things to your remembrance, whatsoever I have said unto you" (John 14:26). This must have been a very comforting thought to Jesus' disciples who were dreading His departure from their midst. The Master was actually saying that they would not be alone, because the Holy Spirit would always be with them, and He would bring to their minds the things that Jesus had taught them. This is one reason why the Holy Spirit is called the Comforter – truly He brings God's comfort to each of us because He is always there.

The comforting presence of the Holy Spirit in our lives draws us ever closer to our Father, and to Jesus.

The Holy Spirit Imparts God's Life to Us

The quickening power of the Holy Spirit in our lives helps us to be strong, vigilant, and active. The Bible says, "But if the Spirit of him that raised up Jesus from the dead dwell in you, he that raised up Christ from the dead shall also quicken your mortal bodies by his Spirit that dwelleth in you" (Rom. 8:11).

The Holy Spirit is the Spirit of God who raised Jesus from the dead. God's Spirit within us gives life, health, and strength to our bodies, and He helps us to know that we are God's children: "The Spirit itself beareth witness with our spirit, that we are the children of God" (Rom. 8:16). It is the Spirit who helps us to know our Father in heaven.

R.A. Torrey shows what happens when we allow the Holy Spirit to work in our lives:

"'Power belongeth unto God.' The Holy Spirit is the Person who imparts to the individual believer the power that belongs to God. The Holy Spirit's work in the believer is to take what belongs to God and make it ours. All the manifold power of God belongs to the children of God as their birthright in Christ; 'All things are yours' (1 Corinthians 3:21). But all that belongs to us as our birthright in Christ becomes ours in actual possession through the Holy Spirit's work in us as individuals."

Oswald Chambers writes: "No power on earth or in hell can conquer the Spirit of God in a human spirit. It is an inner inconquerableness."

"For the law of the Spirit of life in Christ Jesus hath made me free from the law of sin and death" (Rom. 8:2).

The Fruit and Gifts of the Holy Spirit

When we are filled with the Holy Spirit (sent to us by our loving Father), we can enjoy the fruit of the Holy Spirit in all the relationships and responsibilities of our lives. Paul wrote, "But the fruit of the Spirit is love, joy, peace, longsuffering, kindness, goodness, faithfulness, gentleness, self-control. Against such there is no law" (Gal. 5:22-23, NKJV).

These fruits are for us to use and enjoy, and they come to us from our heavenly Father, through the Holy Spirit. As we let them come to fruition in our lives everything changes in positive ways. These fruits are divine attributes, and they describe the character of our Father. He imparts them to us by His Holy Spirit.

As a result of his encounter with the Holy Spirit, an Episcopal clergyman wrote, "Now I know that I am on the right track for the first time in my ministry." He went on to say that through the Holy Spirit he felt "a stronger sense of being guided, of walking a particular appointed path, of being a piece fitting into a glorious huge puzzle, of not being quite so tormented by the apparent dead-ends, of new hope."

Countless others who have been filled with the Holy Spirit and have tasted His fruit and experienced His gifts have echoed this pastor's experience. God's Holy Spirit is there for us at all times, an infinite resource of so many good things from the hand of God.

About the gifts and fruit of the Holy Spirit, R.A. Torrey wrote: "If you desire these graces in your character and in your life, renounce yourself and all your attempts at holiness. Then let the Holy Spirit, who dwells in you, take full control and bear His own glorious fruit. Live in the reality expressed in Galatians 2:20: 'I am crucified with Christ: nevertheless I live; yet not I, but Christ liveth in me: and the life which I now live in the flesh I live by the faith of the Son of God, who loved me, and gave himself for me.'"

Through the Holy Spirit we get to know God as the source of all power for living, witnessing, and being fruitful.

Walk in the Spirit, and you shall not
fulfill the lust of the flesh. For the flesh lusts
against the spirit, and the Spirit against
the flesh; and these are contrary to one
another, so that you do not do the things
that you wish. But if you are led
by the Spirit, you are not under
the law. . . .If we live in the Spirit,
let us also walk in the Spirit.
(Gal. 5:16-25, NKJV).

Prayer of Response: Heavenly Father, I thank you for the precious Holy Spirit who gives me power, boldness, comfort, peace, and so much more. Fill me with the Holy Spirit daily so that I will be able to be a fruitful Christian in all the relationships and responsibilities of my life. Let His power and fruit be manifested in all that I say and do. In Jesus' name I pray, Amen.

PART II

ATTRIBUTES OF GOD

PART II

ATTRIBUTES OF GOD

We have already seen how God is Triune – eternally existent in three Persons – the Father, the Son, and the Holy Spirit. John writes, "No one has seen God at any time. The only begotten Son, who is in the bosom of the Father, He has declared Him" (John 1:18, NKJV).

The Son is the fullness of the Godhead manifested. (See Col. 2:9.) John writes, "And the Word became flesh and dwelt among us, and we beheld His glory, the glory as of the only begotten of the Father, full of grace and truth" (John 1:14, NKJV).

The Holy Spirit has been given to us by the Father and the Son, and He is present with us, taking action in our lives. Paul writes, "But as it is written: 'Eye has not seen, nor ear heard, nor have entered into the heart of man the things which God has prepared for those who love Him.' But God has revealed them to us through His Spirit. For the Spirit searches all things, yes, the deep things of God" (1 Cor. 2:9-10, NKJV).

The deep things of God include His essential attributes, both spiritual and moral.

As we will show in the following chapters, the Father's spiritual attributes include His omnipotence (all-powerfulness), omniscience (all-knowingness), and omnipresence (His presence everywhere). The moral attributes of God include such things as His love, faithfulness, mercy, righteousness, wisdom, truth, peace, and strength.

The attributes we will discuss in this section form the essential, eternal, and unchanging nature of our Father. They are His characteristics, and they define His personality. As we get to know Him better, we experience the benefits of these attributes in our own lives. For example, we learn first-hand that He has the power to heal and to make provision for us. We experience His joy as our strength. We are surrounded by His love. We experience His mercy and righteousness. He gives us His wisdom and truth. We learn that His peace surpasses all understanding.

As you reflect on the attributes of God in the next section of *Knowing God Intimately*, we pray that you will understand more clearly who God is to you, and what He wants to accomplish in you and through you.

4

KNOWING GOD THROUGH HIS LOVE AND FAITHFULNESS

For God so loved the world, that he gave
his only begotten Son, that whosoever
believeth in him should not perish,
but have everlasting life.
(John 3:16)

Our Faithful Father Loves Us
With an Everlasting Love

John writes, "My little children, let us not love in word, neither in tongue; but in deed and in truth" (1 John 3:18). What a revealingly simple sentence this is! It seems clear from this passage that God is quite aware of the ease with which we humans can say, "I love you," without really knowing, or sometimes even caring, what we are really saying. When God talks about love, He is also talking about faithfulness. Love, to Him, is more than emotions and feelings. To God, the foundation of love is covenant – an eternally binding agreement. Real love, the God kind of love, is one of uncompromising and faithful commitment.

True love and faithfulness are inseparable twins. You can't have one without the other.

Love grows deeper with time, as we experience the love and faithfulness of another. The Bible mentions four kinds of love, and the four Greek words for these manifestations of love are *eros, phileo, storge,* and *agape*. The first, *eros*, is sexual, physical, and erotic. This kind of love is romantic in nature, and it may draw a man and woman together into a physical relationship.

Phileo, on the other hand, is brotherly love. This refers to the kind of love that exists between friends, regardless of gender. It is inherent in all friendships.

Storge is the kind of love that family members experience in their relationships with each other. It is the love between parent and child, siblings, and the extended family as well.

The kind of love that God gives is known as *agape* – the noblest love of all. Jesus explained to us that *agape* is God's unconditional, faithful, never-failing love for His children. Through Jesus, the Father has expressed agape-love for all mankind.

The contrast between *agape* and *phileo* is revealed in a poignant story about the time when Peter denied his Master, Jesus. Soon after Peter's denial of Him, Jesus was crucified. Following His resurrection, Jesus encountered Peter. He asked, "Simon, son of Jonah, do you love Me more than these?" (John 21:15, NKJV). Jesus used the word which means *agape* in this passage.

Peter replied, "Yes, Lord; You know that I love You" (John 21:15, NKJV). Peter, unlike Jesus, used the word which means *phileo* in his answer. Having failed the Lord so grievously, Peter's own sense of unworthiness made it seem impossible for him to commit himself to the kind of love Jesus was asking of him. It was not because Peter did not love the Savior deeply; his inability to enter into an *agape* relationship with the Lord was due to the fact that he did not love or trust himself enough to love at the level of faithfulness Jesus was looking for.

This is a problem we all face, and it seems to be an inherent part of the human condition. It is a result of the fall of Adam and Eve. It is hard to love ourselves enough to love others as we ought to do. Conversely, it is hard to love others as we ought to do when, in many ways, we love ourselves more than we ought to do (in the wrong way), in a prideful, narcissistic, self-centered way. Only God, by His faithful Spirit, can impart to us the kind of unselfish, unfailing, faithful love He has commanded us to participate in.

"God is love," (1 John 4:8), and His ". . . faithfulness endures to all generations" (Ps. 119:90). God's love and His faithfulness are inextricably entwined, and these attributes are clearly seen in this passage from the Scriptures: "Being confident of this very thing, that he which hath begun a good work in you will perform it until the day of Jesus Christ" (Phil. 1:6). This is God's love and faithfulness in action in our lives

We pray that you will experience a fuller measure of God's love and faithfulness as you read the following sections of this chapter.

A Letter From the Father to You

Dearly beloved, I love you.[1] My love for you is so great that I gave My only begotten Son to die in place of you.[2] Even though you have never seen Me, I want you to remember always that I dwell within you.[3] Let the love I have for you flow out of you, toward others.[4]

Believe that I love you, because I am love.[5] When you dwell in love, you dwell in Me, and I dwell in you.[6] I love you with an everlasting love, and I have drawn you with My lovingkindness.[7]

Always remember how I showed My love for you, by sending Christ to die for you.[8] Remember, also, that nothing shall ever be able to separate you from My love which you've found in Christ Jesus.[9] Receive My love,[10] and walk in love toward others.[11]

Remember, My child, that all things work together for good in the lives of those who love Me.[12]

Dearly beloved child, I am your faithful Father. What I have spoken to you I will do, and what I have said to you I will make good.[13] Not one word of all My promises to you has ever failed.[14] I will preserve you.[15]

My child, I am your God forever and ever.[16] I will establish you, and I will keep you from all evil.[17] Trust in Me with all your heart, and don't lean upon your own understanding. In all your ways acknowledge Me, and I will direct your paths.[18]

My child, cast all your care upon Me, because I will always care about you.[19] I will always deal well with you, My child, according to My Word.[20]

I am never slack concerning My promises, beloved child.[21] All of My promises are Yes and Amen in Christ Jesus.[22]

References: (1) 1 John 4:10; (2) John 3:16; (3) 1 John 4:16; (4) Mark 12:30-33; (5) 1 John 4:8; (6) 1 John 4:12; (7) Jeremiah 31:3; (8) Romans 5:8; (9) Romans 8:38-39; (10) Romans 5:8; (11) Ephesians 5:2; (12) Romans 8:28;

(13) Numbers 23:19; (14) 1 Kings 8:56; (15) Psalms 31:23; (16) Psalms 48:14; (17) 2 Thessalonians 3:3; (18) Proverbs 3:5-6; (19) 1 Peter 5:7; (20) Psalms 13:6; (21) 2 Peter 3:9; (22) 2 Corinthians 1:20.

God Is Love

It is God's amazing love for us that leads us to Him in the first place. The fact that He gave His only begotten Son (Jesus) to be the sacrifice for our sins is almost incomprehensible. Such love has no human parallel, for what earthly father would willingly give his only son as a sacrifice for the sins of others?

D.L. Moody wrote, "After I became a father and woke up to the realization of what it cost God to have His Son die, I began to see that God was to be loved just as much as His Son was. Why, it took more love for God to give His Son to die than it would to die Himself. You would a thousand times sooner die yourself in your son's place than have him taken away. If the executioner were about to take your son to the gallows, you would say, 'Let me die in his stead; let my son be spared.' Oh, think of the love God must have had for this world, that he gave His only begotten Son to die for it! And that is what I want you to understand. 'The Father himself loves you because you have loved me.' If a man has loved Christ, God will set His love upon him."

It is this compelling love that motivates us to love God and others. The Bible says, "We love him because he first loved us" (1 John 4:19).

The Father's love for us is truly overwhelming. It is an extremely important route to knowing Him. In fact, the Apostle John writes, "Beloved, let us love one another: for love is of God; and every one that loveth is born of God, and knoweth God. He that loveth not knoweth not God; for God is love" (1 John 4:7-8).

To know God, therefore, is to love Him, and this impels us to love others as well. The love we have to give reveals how extensive our knowledge of God actually is. Those who do not or cannot love do not know God, for He is love. Those who are able to practice love toward God and their fellow-man have been born of God and know God.

Through Jesus Christ we experience the Father's love. Throughout history nothing has revealed to Christians the love of God like the cross of Christ. God's Son hung on a cross and died for us. That is love. God loved us long before we knew Him. This was His plan from the beginning. He loved us before we ever thought of loving Him. Parents love their children before the children know about their parents' love, and long before we were even born, we were in God's thoughts. God told Jeremiah, "Before I formed thee in the belly, I knew thee" (Jer. 1:5).

A middle-aged man had a very difficult time experiencing and giving love. He went to his counselor who was able to help him see that some of his problems had stemmed from the fact that this man had never once heard his earthly father say, "I love you."

Because of this lack, the counselor prayed, "Father, bridge the gap between the love this man should have received from his dad, and the love he actually did receive," and he began to work with him on a weekly basis.

It took a long time for the counselee to discover that his heavenly Father loved him, but he explained the process this way: "Jesus became the bridge between my desire to love and be loved, and God's desire to help me know His love and His desire to receive my love. Through Jesus' many acts of selfless love I was able to get a picture of the Father's great love for me. He drew me to the Father, and my frozen heart was thawed."

Later, this same individual visited his dying father in the hospital. He went over to him and said, "Dad, I love you," then he gently stroked his forehead. With tears in his eyes, the father weakly replied, "I love you too, son."

Both men wept and embraced, and the son was able to lead his father to Jesus. Starved for love all their lives, both men found their fulfillment in the love of their heavenly Father.

God's love knows no bounds. Nothing, except our own bad choices, can prevent us from being the recipients of His great love. The Bible says, "Who shall separate us from the love of Christ? Shall tribulation, or distress, or persecution, or famine, or nakedness, or peril, or sword?" (Rom. 8:35). No, in all these things we are more than conquerors! (See Rom. 8:37.)

God's love is a generous and lavish love. His love has no conditions. It is a self-giving love which God offers to people. Because it is God's love, there are no limits to its magnitude or operation.

Knowing God Through His Faithfulness

Jeremiah wrote, "Through the Lord's mercies we are not consumed, because His compassions fail not. They are new every morning; Great is Your faithfulness" (Lam. 3:22-23, NKJV).

Again, the Bible links the amazing love of God with His incredible faithfulness in our lives. His compassion (love) never fails. (See also 1 Cor. 13.) His mercies are new to us each morning. His faithfulness is greater than we know. Because God is love, and His love is perfect, He cannot be unfaithful in any way.

On nearly every page of the holy Scriptures we find God's promises engraved. He means for us to reap, claim, and appropriate these promises for ourselves and every member of our family. The pages of the Bible declare the Father's faithfulness to His children. Because He is faithful and true, He always does what He says He will do.

What does the Word of God tell us about the eternal faithfulness of our Father? Here are several promises related to His faithfulness:

"Faithful is he that calleth you, who also will do it" (1 Thess. 5:24). God has called us, and He will be faithful to accomplish His purposes in our life, including His goal for us to get to know Him intimately.

"And, behold, I am with thee, and will keep thee in all places whither thou goest, and will bring thee again into this land; for I will not leave thee, until I have done that which I have spoken to thee of" (Gen. 28:15). God is with us. God will keep us. He will bring us into the Promised Land. He will finish His work in our lives.

"Know therefore that the Lord thy God, he is God, the faithful God, which keepeth covenant and mercy with them that love him and keep his commandments to a thousand generations" (Deut. 7:9). God is not saying here that His covenant-love and mercy are conditional upon our keeping His laws. Rather, He is saying His unconditional faithfulness cannot be fully received or enjoyed in a condition of disobedience.

"Thy mercy, O Lord, is in the heavens; and thy faithfulness reacheth unto the clouds" (Ps. 36:5). The height of God's faithfulness cannot be measured.

"I will sing of the mercies of the Lord for ever: with my mouth will I make known thy faithfulness to all generations. For I have said, Mercy shall be built up for ever: thy faithfulness shalt thou establish in the very heavens" (Ps. 89:1-2). God's faithfulness is for all generations, and it is established in heaven. We receive it as we become aware of it, believe it, and move closer to that intimate fellowship which enables us to more fully apprehend and experience it.

The Prerequisite Is Trust

A famous pastor said, "Don't try to hold God's hand; let Him hold yours. Let Him do the holding, and you do the trusting." Little children feel secure when their hand is held by their father. As they place a tiny hand in their father's much larger hand, peace is imparted from the father to the child.

Children trust their father to guide, guard, and protect them. It is the trust that issues from innocence, genuineness, and faith. It springs from a loving relationship between the father and his child.

In our relationship with our heavenly Father we must become like trusting little children, as Jesus pointed out: "Assuredly, I say to you, unless you are converted and become as little children, you will by no means enter the kingdom of heaven. Therefore whoever humbles himself as this little child is the greatest in the kingdom of heaven" (Matt. 18:3-4, NKJV).

It is sometimes difficult for us to have a child-like attitude as we grow older. We tend to think that we are "all grown up now." But, in God's eyes, we are always His precious children. He loves for us to place our hand in His and to let Him love us and take care of us. As we do this, we come to know Him better.

Paul admonished Timothy to "Trust. . .in the living God" (1 Tim. 6:17). Trusting is the key to receiving the promises of God in our lives. Trusting in God's faithfulness helps us to grow in our knowledge of God.

God loves us, and He is faithful in meeting all of our needs, just as He promised. He is worthy of our trust.

A young man who had been a male prostitute in New York City for many years in order to support his drug habit heard a street preacher loudly proclaiming the gospel message. This handsome youth had a mind which was like a blank slate because he had used hallucinogenic drugs for so long. He heard the minister ask, "Do you want to meet Jesus?" The preacher then invited all of those within earshot to a church service that evening.

The young man thought, "I want to meet Jesus. I'll go to church." He thought that Jesus himself would be standing behind the pulpit, preaching.

Nervously, he crept into the sanctuary that evening. The minister was preaching an evangelistic message, and at the conclusion, he invited those who wanted to meet Jesus to come forward. The youth literally tore out of his seat and ran to the front of the church. He wanted to meet Jesus!

Still thinking that Jesus might be in a different room, he followed the personal worker to the prayer room. It was there that he discovered Jesus in all of His fullness, gave his heart to Him, repented of his sins, and determined to follow Jesus for the rest of his life.

Diligently, the young man studied the Word of God. He attended church every time the doors were open, and sought Christian fellowship at every possible opportunity. God healed his drug-damaged mind and began to prepare him for Christian ministry.

A couple of years later, this new believer prepared to go to Bible college in order to study for Christian ministry. He wrote down a list of items he would need to take to school with him.

A few days later the youth pastor and his wife invited the future minister to dinner. They said, "Cody, we have a few things we've put aside for you. Many of these things were duplicate gifts we received for our wedding, and we thought you could use them."

To his amazement, Cody found that the things the couple had put aside were the exact things he had put on his list. God was faithful in meeting each of his needs.

God loves you, and He cares about every detail of your life.

Now to Him who is able to do exceedingly
abundantly above all that we ask or think,
according to the power that works in us,
to Him be glory in the church
by Christ Jesus to all generations,
forever and ever. Amen.
(Eph. 3:20-21, NKJV)

Prayer Response: Loving and faithful Father, how I rejoice in the truth that nothing shall ever be able to separate me from your love. Great is your faithfulness to me, Father, and every day I experience new mercies from your hands. Thank you for loving me and taking good care of me. Thank you for fulfilling your promises in my life, and for supplying all of my needs. In Jesus' name, Amen.

5

KNOWING GOD THROUGH HIS MERCY AND RIGHTEOUSNESS

But God, who is rich in mercy, because of His great love with which He loved us.
(Eph. 2:4, NKJV)

We Find Righteousness Through God's Mercy

Our God is both merciful and righteous. It is His mercy toward us that prevents us from getting what we deserve as a result of our sins. The righteousness of God is revealed through His great and tender mercies toward us.

"For the wages of sin is death, but the gift of God is eternal life in Christ Jesus our Lord" (Rom. 6:23, NKJV).

Both His righteousness and mercy are manifestations of God's holiness. God's righteousness causes Him always to do what is right, and this is revealed in His punishment of the wicked, His forgiveness of those who repent, keeping His promises, delivering His people from the wicked, and rewarding those who are made righteous in Christ.

Through His mercy God reveals His full lovingkindness toward us, His children. "For thou, Lord, art good, and ready to forgive; and plenteous in mercy unto all them that call upon thee" (Ps. 86:5).

When Adam and Eve sinned in the Garden of Eden, the Bible tells us that their eyes were opened and they saw that they were naked. Prior to this "enlightenment," they had been clothed in the glory of God; now the glory was gone. (See Gen. 3:7.)

Previously, they had been secure in their relationship with God and each other. Now, however, they felt overwhelmed by a sense of loss, fear, shame, and guilt before God. Instead of running to God with repentant hearts and seeking His forgiveness, they hid in fear. They hid themselves, ". . .from the presence of the Lord God amongst the trees of the garden" (Gen. 3:8).

We have inherited this same fallen nature that seeks to blame others, to hide from God, and to cover our faults in our own way. Children, for example, usually don't run to their parents for comfort and acceptance when they know they've done something wrong. Instead, they may try to hide from them or at least to hide their misdeeds from them.

When we sin, it seems natural for us to want to hide it from God and others, and we sometimes even try to "hide" it from ourselves through denial. How ridiculous this is, to think that we can hide anything from our all-knowing and all-seeing God. He knew us even before we were born! (See Jer. 1:5.)

Too often we may try to run from God rather than running to Him in order to receive His mercy and to benefit from His righteousness. The "fig-leaf aprons" we create may include our jobs, our financial resources, service in any form, or anything we may perceive to be an accomplishment. Such things will help us to feel good about ourselves.

The better way, of course, is to go to God in humility, repenting of our sin, and receiving and accepting His mercy in the form of forgiveness and cleansing from unrighteousness. Then, through faith, we are able to cast all our cares upon Him and to let Him be God in our lives.

In order to know God intimately, we must get rid of all the "fig leaves" we've created to hide any part of our lives from our holy Father. It is Jesus alone that enables us to become righteous in Him. (See 1 Cor. 1:30.)

One of the most important questions we must ask ourselves as we seek to know God intimately is: Why do I think I can take better care of myself than can God, who created me and loves me more than I love myself?

In this chapter you will discover how God imparts His righteousness to us, and how His mercy is involved in our daily lives. May you sing of the mercies of the Lord forever, and experience His righteousness every day of your life.

A Letter From the Father to You

My child, I am a God of mercy, and I will not turn My face away from you.[1] I am always ready to pardon you.[2] My mercy toward you is everlasting.[3] As the heaven is high above the earth, so is My mercy great toward you.[4]

Beloved, My mercy endures forever.[5] I beseech you, by My mercies toward you, to present yourself as a living sacrifice to Me. Do not allow yourself to be conformed to this world, but be transformed by the renewing of your mind so that you will be able to prove My good, perfect, and acceptable will.[6]

Dear child, I brought you out of darkness and the shadow of death. I broke your bonds asunder. These are only some of My mercies toward you.[7] I sent My Word and healed you, and I delivered you from all your destructions.[8]

As your God, I want you to know that I am righteous in all My ways, and holy in all My works.[9]

My beloved child, I made Jesus, who knew no sin, to be sin for you, so that you might be made My righteousness in Him.[10] I made Jesus to be your wisdom, righteousness, sanctification, and redemption.[11] May you always be found in Him, not having your own righteousness, which is of the law, but My righteousness which comes to you through faith.[12]

I will lead you in the paths of righteousness.[13] My eyes are upon you, and My ears are always open to your cry.[14] Your steps are ordered by Me, and I delight in the way you've chosen.[15] I have a reward for the righteous.[16]

My child, I will withhold no good thing from you as you walk in righteousness.[17] In righteousness you will be established.[18] Always remember that righteousness belongs to Me.[19] I will always be your righteousness.[20]

References: (1) Deuteronomy 4:31; (2) Nehemiah 9:17; (3) Psalms 107:1; (4) Psalms 103:11; (5) Psalms 107:1; (6) Romans 12:1-2; (7) Psalms 107:14; (8) Psalms 107:20; (9) Psalms 145:17; (10) 2 Corinthians 5:21; (11) 1 Corinthians 1:30; (12) Philippians 3:9; (13) Psalms 23:3; (14) Psalms 34:15; (15) Psalms 37:23; (16) Psalms 58:11; (17) Psalms 84:11; (18) Isaiah 54:14; (19) Daniel 9:7; (20) Philippians 3:9.

God Is Merciful

Mercy is a quality of compassion and forbearance shown by God toward sinners and believers alike. It is a quality that is not natural to human beings, but it is a divine attribute that leads our heavenly Father to forgive us of our sins when we do earnestly repent of them and humble ourselves in His presence.

Our God is merciful (full of mercy), and His mercy extends to sinners as well as saints. The Psalmist describes this attribute of our Father's personality for us: "For thou, Lord, art good, and ready to forgive, and plenteous in mercy to all them that call upon thee" (Ps. 86:5). God manifested His mercy toward sinners through the death of His Son, Jesus Christ.

Through Christ we are able to receive God's mercy as we repent of our sins. Listen to how Isaiah describes this aspect of the Father's mercy: "Let the wicked forsake his way, and the unrighteous man his thoughts: and let him return unto the Lord, and he will have mercy upon him; and to our God, for he will abundantly pardon" (Isa. 55:7).

God is plenteous in mercy, and He will abundantly pardon. God's mercy is revealed through the pardoning of our sins. His promise is there for all to act upon: "The Lord your God is gracious and merciful, and will not turn away his face from you, if you return unto him" (2 Chron. 30:9).

God's mercy is everlasting – it never ends. The Psalmist writes, "His mercy is everlasting" (Ps. 100:5). Mercy is a deeply ingrained part of our Father's personality: "Thou, O Lord, art a God full of compassion, and gracious, longsuffering, and plenteous in mercy and truth" (Ps. 86:15).

How big is God's mercy toward us? Again, the Psalmist gives a vivid description of the Father's great mercy: "As the heaven is high above the earth, so great is his mercy toward them that fear him" (Ps. 103:11).

It is because of His great mercies to us that we are called to present our bodies as a living sacrifice to Him, as Paul beseeches us to do. (See Rom. 12:1-2.) Truly, this is our reasonable service – the least that we can do – in response to His great mercy toward us. The Father's mercy toward us impelled Him to give His only begotten Son as the sacrifice for our sins. Jesus willingly laid down His life for us. Our reasonable response to such great mercy is to lay down our lives for Him, especially since that is the pathway to our own victory and blessing.

Paul further admonishes us to stop being conformed to this world. Rather, we are to be transformed by the renewing of our mind, so that God's perfect will may be revealed to us, in us, and through us. This is possible because of God's mercy toward us. "With the Lord there is mercy" (Ps. 130:7).

Enduring Mercy

An anonymous writer helps us to see the relationship between God's enduring mercy and His other attributes. "*God's laws* are inviolable, sacred, not to be broken. *God's standards* are changeless. *God's judgments* are inevitable, unavoidable, certain. *God's love* is limitless, steadfast. *God's promises* are sure, trustworthy. *God's mercy* endureth forever."

One of the greatest aspects of God's mercy is that He wants to communicate with us, His people. This is one of the things that makes Christianity different from all the other world religions. Our God wants to have fellowship with us. In no other religion does its deity offer such a uniquely vital relationship. The fellowship He offers is the most intimate kind, for He comes and abides within our hearts by the Holy Spirit.

Therefore, Christianity is not a religion. It is a relationship that is based on God's mercy toward sinners and saints. This marvelous relationship begins with mercy, is sustained by mercy, and continues on through mercy. How big is God's mercy? It is big enough to satisfy all the longings of the human soul.

Mercy tells us that God is *for* us, God is *with* us, and God is *in* us. Mercy tells us that God cares about us – both for our spiritual and physical needs. Mercy tells us that God is speaking to those who are still enough to listen for His voice. Mercy tells us that we are created in the very image of our Father.

Our God Is Righteous

R.C. Sproul writes, "God's justice is never divorced from His righteousness. He never condemns the innocent. He never clears the guilty. He never punishes with undo severity. He never fails to reward righteousness. His justice is perfect justice."

One of the most amazing miracles in the Bible – a divine act of mercy — is the one that Paul describes in his second letter to the Corinthians: "For he hath made him [Jesus] to be sin for us, who knew no sin; that we might be made the righteousness of God in him" (2 Cor. 5:21). On the cross, Jesus Christ took upon himself all the sins of humanity, and in this sense He became sin for us. He took our sins upon himself, because He was the sacrifice for our sins, the Lamb of God ". . .who takes away the sin of the world" (John 1:29, NKJV).

In the same way that we are able to experience healing through the stripes of Jesus and know peace through Him, we are able to experience the mercy and righteousness of God only through Christ Jesus.

Righteousness includes being in right relationship with God, acting in accord with God's laws, and living free from the power of sin. This can only be achieved through faith in Jesus Christ. Paul wrote, "But of him are ye in Christ Jesus, who of God is made unto us wisdom, and righteousness, and sanctification, and redemption" (1 Cor. 1:30).

Our God is righteous in His forgiving of our sins as well as in His punishment of the wicked. In fact, His righteousness and justice guarantee us that He will forgive us of our sins when we confess them to Him. (See 1 John 1:9.)

The righteousness of God makes it certain that He will keep all of His promises to His children. Again, His righteousness guarantees that He will keep His Word to us, and fulfill all of His promises.

It is God's righteousness that enables Him to be our Defender and Vindicator when enemies come against us. David wrote, "Many a time have they afflicted me. . .yet they have not prevailed against me. . . . The

Lord is righteous: he hath cut asunder the cords of the wicked" (Ps. 129:1-4). This He will do for us as well, because He is our righteous God.

God's righteousness leads Him to reward the righteous. Our righteous Father will never allow His righteous children to go unrewarded. He guarantees that He will reward us as, when, and after we walk in righteousness.

Jehovah-Tsidkenu

The Hebrew words *Jehovah-Tsidkenu* literally mean "the Lord God is our righteousness," and it was Jeremiah, the prophet, who spelled this out for us. He wrote during a time when the people of God were being scattered hither and yon, in violation of God's plan for Israel. He promised, "But I will gather the remnant of My flock out of all countries where I have driven them, and bring them back to their folds; and they shall be fruitful and increase. I will set up shepherds over them who will feed them; and they shall fear no more, nor be dismayed, nor shall they be lacking" (Jer. 23:3-4, NKJV).

The next section of this scriptural passage is a messianic prophecy about Jesus becoming our righteousness: "Behold, the days are coming, says the Lord, that I will raise to

David a Branch of righteousness; a King shall reign and prosper, and execute judgment and righteousness in the earth. In His days Judah will be saved, and Israel will dwell safely; now this is His name by which He will be called: THE LORD OUR RIGHTEOUSNESS" (Jer. 23:5-6, NKJV).

God is our righteousness through Jesus Christ, and this is why Paul wrote, "And be found in him [Jesus], not having mine own righteousness, which is of the law, but that which is through the faith of Christ, the righteousness which is of God by faith" (Phil. 3:9). Righteousness is of God, and it becomes ours through faith in Christ's atoning work.

Hal Lindsay wrote, "We should make it our aim to trust Christ to work in us a life of righteousness. We all grow in this, so don't get discouraged or forget that God accepts us as we are. He wants our hearts to be constantly set toward pleasing Him and have faith to trust Him to help us."

Hunger for Righteousness

The human race is starved for righteousness, because no matter how hard people try, they cannot find righteousness on their own. Isaiah said, "All our righteousnesses are as filthy rags" (Isa. 64:6).

A thirty-year-old Christian named Philip felt burnt out, frustrated, and depressed. He told his counselor, "All my life I've tried so hard to do what is right, but I keep falling down. I'm just a total failure. I'll never know success."

The counselor responded, "Phil, what's this talk about success? You're a failure to begin with!" He went on to explain that it is only through Jesus Christ that we can truly accomplish anything, and he gave Phil the Scripture: "Without Me [Jesus] you can do nothing" (John 15:5, NKJV).

At first, Philip felt hurt, shocked and defensive when he heard the counselor's seemingly harsh words, but on his way home and throughout the following week he kept hearing them echo in his heart: "You're a failure to begin with!"

The more he thought about it, the more he realized it was true. "I am a failure to begin with. Why am I striving for success? I am going to learn to trust God instead of always trying so hard. I am going to trust His grace and mercy for the righteousness I need."

As this realization dawned on him, the heavy sense of depression and frustration lifted. He said, "This was one of the happiest moments of my life. I don't have to do it all on my own. I learned to do my best and to let God do the rest."

Phil had discovered that his righteousness was worthless. All his endeavors to live right through sheer determination had always resulted in failure. His will power was not enough. Though he had known this Scripture all of his life, it finally became an actual reality to him: "I can do all things *through Christ* who strengthens me" (Phil. 4:13, NKJV).

No person (other than Jesus Christ) has ever succeeded in keeping all the Law of God. No person has been able to adhere to all the Ten Commandments. For this reason Paul wrote, "Therefore the law was our tutor to bring us to Christ, that we might be justified by faith" (Gal. 3:24, NKJV). The justification spoken of here has two connotations: one, the forgiveness of sin and the removal of its guilt and punishment; two, the imputation of Christ's righteousness and restoration to God's favor.

Our inability to keep the Law shows us that we need a Savior, so we turn to Jesus Christ who is the righteousness of God revealed on earth. As we place our faith and trust in Him, His righteousness is imparted to us, and our hunger for righteousness is fulfilled, as Jesus himself promised it would be: "Blessed are they which do hunger and thirst after righteousness: for they shall be filled" (Matt. 5:6).

Our hunger for righteousness is our hunger for God.

The Paths of Righteousness

To walk on the paths of righteousness is to walk in the footsteps of God. "For to this you were called, because Christ also suffered for us, leaving us an example, that you should follow His steps: 'Who committed no sin, nor was deceit found in His mouth,' who, when He was reviled, did not revile in return; when He suffered, He did not threaten, but committed Himself to Him who judges righteously; who Himself bore our sins in His own body on the tree, that we, having died to sins, might live for righteousness – by whose stripes you were healed" (1 Pet. 2:21-24, NKJV).

God has called us to a life of righteousness, and He has made it possible for us to walk in righteousness, because Jesus took our sins upon himself on the cross. Now, dead to our sins, we are able to live for righteousness, because the cross of Jesus Christ has completely set us free!

It is God who leads us in the paths of righteousness for His name's sake. (See Ps. 23:3.)

He promises, "The steps of a good man are ordered by the Lord: and he [God] delighteth in his way" (Ps. 37:23).

Righteousness and judgment are the habitation of his throne.
(Ps. 97:2)

Prayer Response: Merciful and righteous Father, I thank you for your great mercies to me. Through Jesus, who knew no sin, I have been made righteous before you. Thank you for imparting your righteousness to me. I ask for your continuing mercies in my life to enable me to walk in mercy and righteousness for as long as I shall live. In Jesus' name I pray, Amen.

6

KNOWING GOD THROUGH HIS WISDOM AND TRUTH

*Wisdom is the principal thing; therefore
get wisdom: and with all thy
getting get understanding.*
(Prov. 4:7)

Wisdom Knows How to Apply God's Truth

God is revealed in His Word as the source of all wisdom and truth, two more of His essential attributes. There are two things that God cannot do – He cannot lie, and He cannot fail. He wants us to walk in His wisdom and truth. "So teach us to number our days, that we may apply our hearts unto wisdom" (Ps. 90:12), says the Psalmist, knowing that, as we walk in God's wisdom, truth will preserve us from failure.

There is a vast difference between wisdom and knowledge, and God's wisdom is far superior to worldly knowledge. The Bible says, "The wisdom of this world is foolishness with God" (1 Cor. 3:19).

Wisdom stems from truth. Wisdom applies the truth of God to a given situation, and it is God's truth that ". . .shall be thy shield and buckler" (Ps. 91:4).

The Word of God is a book of truth. (See Ps. 119:142.) The Holy Spirit is the Spirit of truth. (See 1 John 5:6.) Jesus is the Truth. (See John 14:6.) As we continue in the knowledge of God's truth, it makes us free. (See John 8:32.) In order for the truth to become reality, it must be believed and trusted enough to be acted upon.

Can you see what precious commodities God has given us in His truth and wisdom? He has made Jesus to be wisdom, righteousness, sanctification, and redemption unto us. In short, everything we need is found in Jesus, and we have been given the Holy Spirit to reveal all this to us. Our enemy, however, is the deceiver, and he will always endeavor to keep the Jesus of the Word from becoming reality in our lives by playing on our emotions, whispering lies to our minds, and encouraging us to focus on ourselves, our needs, our abilities, and doing our own thing. In these ways, he can keep us from gaining the level of understanding that will cause God's Word to become wisdom and produce faith in our lives. What a tragedy a lack of faith is. Without faith intimacy with God is not possible, because we come into His presence by faith. (See Heb. 11:6.)

In this exciting chapter you will see how God's wisdom and truth apply to your daily life. As you learn to walk in His wisdom and truth, windows of understanding will open, allowing fresh winds to stir your heart to seek a deeper walk with your God.

A Letter From the Father to You

My child, nothing you desire can be compared with wisdom.[1] Length of days are in wisdom's right hand, and riches and honor are found in wisdom's left hand.[2] The ways of wisdom are ways of pleasantness, and all its paths are peace.[3] My wisdom is a tree of life to all who lay hold upon her.[4]

My child, do not forsake My wisdom. It will preserve you. Love My wisdom, and it will keep you.[5] Wisdom is the principal thing. Therefore, get wisdom, My child, and with all your getting be sure to get understanding as well.[6] When you embrace wisdom, it will bring you to honor.[7]

My truth endures to all generations.[8] My Word is true from the very beginning.[9] All My counsels of old are faithfulness and truth.[10]

It is through My truth that I am able to sanctify you.[11] Everyone who is born of the truth is able to hear My voice.[12] The truth is found in Jesus.[13] Therefore, My precious child, I ask you to think on things that are true, honest, just, pure, lovely, and of good report.[14] Remember, it is the Spirit who bears witness, because the Spirit is truth.[15]

Dearly beloved child, I have no greater joy than to know you are walking in truth.[16]

References: *(1) Proverbs 3:15; (2) Proverbs 3:16; (3) Proverbs 3:17; (4) Proverbs 3:18; (5) Proverbs 4:6; (6) Proverbs 4:7; (7) Proverbs 4:8; (8) Psalms 117:2; (9) Psalms 119:160; (10) Isaiah 25:1; (11) John 17:17; (12) John 18:37; (13) John 14:6; (14) Philippians 4:8; (15) 1 John 5:6; (16) 3 John 4.*

A Never-Failing Fountain of Wisdom

The Bible says, "The fear of the Lord is the beginning of wisdom, and the knowledge of the Holy One is understanding" (Prov. 9:10, NKJV). To fear God is to respect Him with a reverential awe – to honor Him as our awesome, Almighty God. This, the Bible says, is when wisdom begins, and in order to gain spiritual understanding we must get to know Him, for knowing God as the Holy One brings understanding to our hearts. The beginning of wisdom, therefore, is also the beginning of our relationship with our heavenly Father.

J.I. Packer writes, "God's almighty wisdom is always active and never fails. All His works of creation and providence and grace display it, and until we can see it in them, we just are not seeing them straight. But we can't recognize God's wisdom unless we know the end for which He is working." The end which God has in mind is that we would know Him in all His wisdom and understanding.

God, who is wisdom, wants us to experience His wisdom in our lives. That's why He says, "Wisdom is better than rubies" (Prov. 8:11), and God tells us to: ". . .number our days, that we may apply our hearts unto wisdom" (Ps. 90:12).

Wisdom stems from knowing God. As we get to know Him better, we understand that His wisdom never fails. In fact, He says, "Counsel is mine, and sound wisdom: I am understanding; I have strength" (Prov. 8:14). There is a clear connection between God's wisdom, understanding, and strength, and all of these divine attributes are imparted to us when we walk in close communion with our Father.

Wisdom is a fountain that never fails, because it flows from our Father's heart to ours. The Bible says, "Understanding is a wellspring of life unto him that hath it: but the instruction of fools is folly" (Prov. 16:22).

God's Wisdom Reveals His Will to Us

The Bible is a book of wisdom. It reveals the Father's will to us. In its pages we find wisdom, strength, understanding, and life.

The Bible says, "How much better it is to get wisdom than gold! And to get understanding rather to be chosen than silver! The highway of the upright is to depart from evil: he that keepeth his way preserveth his soul" (Prov. 16:16-17). As we walk in the wisdom He gives, we honor Him, and become candidates to receive more of His wisdom.

This is wisdom – to know God's ways and to keep them. There is a direct relationship between our obedience and the impartation of God's wisdom to us, as the following verses declare. Wisdom involves understanding the precepts of God, and this enables us to talk about all His wondrous works with others. (See Ps. 119:27.) Through wisdom we are able to understand God's ways, and this understanding will enable us to walk in His paths. (See Ps. 119:34.)

Knowing God as our Creator helps us to apprehend God's wisdom. Through spiritual understanding we apply His wisdom to our lives. (See Ps. 119:73.) God's commandments abide within the hearts of those who know Him, and this makes them wiser than all their enemies. (See Ps. 119:98.)

The teachings of God's wisdom are found in His Word. Through His Word, therefore, we gain spiritual understanding, and we learn to hate every false way that we find in the world. (See Ps. 119:104.) God's Word sheds the light of wisdom on our path as we make our way through this dark and dying world. (See Ps. 119:105.) We are servants of the great King, who desires to impart His wisdom to us. (See Ps. 119:125.)

The preceding verses we've cited from Psalm 119 are in the form of a prayer that the Psalmist earnestly used in his efforts to get to know God better. As he prayed, he kept coming back to the importance of the Word of God which enables us to get to know God and His wisdom more fully.

Wisdom Imparts Life

The Bible says, "Wisdom giveth life to them that have it" (Eccles. 7:12). Spiritual wisdom begets spiritual life. Joni Eareckson Tada writes, "God's thoughts – at least many of them – *are* within grasp. And when we lay hold of Him and His ideas, then and only then can we be drawn closer to Him." This is how wisdom gives life to us. God's Word is the living book of our living God, and through it He imparts life to those who heed its teachings.

This is one reason why we should seek wisdom, as the Bible admonishes us to do: "If any of you lack wisdom, let him ask of God, that giveth to all men liberally, and upbraideth not; and it shall be given him" (James 1:5). Clearly, God wants us to possess His wisdom, because He knows it will give to us the life and spiritual understanding that come from knowing Him.

We need a greater wisdom than our own to guide us. Only God has the complete plan. Only God knows the future. We need to trust Him to guide us each step of the way. "Trust in the Lord with all your heart, and lean not on your own understanding; in all your ways acknowledge Him, and He shall direct your paths. Do not be wise in your own eyes; fear the Lord and depart from evil. It will be health to your flesh, and strength to your bones" (Prov. 3:5-8, NKJV). As we trust God, in close relationship with Him, we learn not to lean upon our own understanding. We soon discover, as we get closer to the Father, that being wise in our own eyes is foolish. God's wisdom results in health, strength, and life to us.

Countless times during our Christian walk we have not known what to do about a problem or situation. We felt that we needed God's wisdom in order to make the right decision. In those times we stood on the promise of Proverbs 3:5-6 and asked God for wisdom. Over and over again God answered and showed us what to do. Sometimes we waited minutes or hours or at the most just a few days before that answer came, but it always came. Our God is so faithful. As the song says, we have proved Him o'er and o'er.

Several years ago our children were attending a very fine public school system. Our daughter, Varsi, was a junior in high school and our son, Chris, was in the eighth grade in middle school. Both had done well and we were pleased with the schools in every way.

Several weeks into his eighth-grade year, Chris began acting in ways that concerned us. He seemed to be struggling with life and was not as respectful and happy as had been normal for him.

The situation got progressively worse until we knew something had to be done. Should we leave him in the public school and try to work things out, or should we transfer him to a Christian school where the environment might be better for him?

We prayed and asked God for wisdom. Within a few days, both of us agreed that God seemed to be leading us to transfer Chris to the Christian school, which we did. The change in Chris was amazing. Within two or three weeks he was a totally different person.

He was happier, respectful and fun to be around again. God had promised to give us wisdom when we asked Him for it, and He surely did so.

Steps to Wisdom

To receive God's wisdom we must pray for it. (See James 1:5.)

To receive God's wisdom we must pray in faith and not waver. (See James 1:6.)

To receive God's wisdom we must reverence and respect Him. (See Ps. 111:10.)

To receive God's wisdom we must study His Word. (See Prov. 4:5.)

To receive God's wisdom, its life and favor, we must learn to wait and listen. (See Prov. 8:34-35.)

To receive God's wisdom we must get to know Him: "That the God of our Lord Jesus Christ, the Father of glory, may give to you the spirit of wisdom and revelation in the knowledge of Him, the eyes of your understanding being enlightened; that you may know what is the hope of His calling, what are the riches of the glory of His inheritance in the saints, and what is the exceeding greatness of His power toward us who believe, according to the working of His mighty power" (Eph. 1:17-19, NKJV).

God Is True

The Bible tells us, "God is true" (John 3:33). To know the truth, therefore, is to know Him. Great freedom comes to us when we know God as truth. Jesus said, "If ye continue in my word, then are ye my disciples indeed; and ye shall know the truth, and the truth shall make you free" (John 8:32). It is impossible to know the full truth about life without knowing God both intimately and personally.

In his letter to the Romans Paul writes, "Let God be true, but every man a liar" (Rom. 3:4). Jesus said something similar, "He who has received His testimony has certified that God is true" (John 3:33). Our God is true, and ". . .all the promises of God in Him [Jesus] are Yes, and in Him Amen, to the glory of God through us" (2 Cor. 1:20, NKJV). God, who is true and cannot lie, has revealed His truth to us in a variety of ways: through His Son, Jesus Christ; though His Holy Spirit; and through His dynamic Word.

God's Word Is Truth

One of the many ways in which we get to know God is through His Word, by studying it, memorizing it, praying it, meditating upon it, and living it. It is the truth of God's Word that guides our lives. Jesus said to God, the Father, "Thy word is truth" (John 17:17).

We must do more than read the Word as we would a school textbook, as a mere intellectual exercise. God's Word is meant to be fed upon, chewed, swallowed, digested, and thought upon – over and over again. It is the living Word. We must receive the Word into our hearts and allow it to become a part of us.

The Psalmist said something similar to God, "Thy law is the truth" (Ps. 119:142). The truths of God's Word are the meat of our daily lives; they give us strength, health, and direction. They reveal God's will to us. They are the most important words ever written.

"Thy word is true from the beginning" (Ps. 119:160), the Psalmist wrote, and it will be the truth forever, as Jesus pointed out, "Heaven and earth shall pass away, but my words shall not pass away" (Matt. 24:35).

The Bible is God's Word to us in every respect. It contains a revelation of God as He truly is so that we can get to know Him in truth. The ideas and concepts it presents come directly from the heart of God, and He makes himself responsible for every word and promise it contains.

The God of truth wrote the Word of truth so that we could find freedom through Christ who is the truth.

Our God is so holy and righteous that He will personally hasten to perform His Word in our lives. (See Jer. 1:12.) In another place He tells us that all of His Words will accomplish what He has sent them to do. (See Isa. 55:11.)

Whatsoever things are true, whatsoever things are honest, whatsoever things are just, whatsoever things are pure, whatsoever things are lovely, whatsoever things are of good report; if there be any virtue, and if there be any praise, think on these things.
(Phil. 4:8)

Prayer Response: Heavenly Father, thank you for all the promises of your Word which proclaim that I will always be able to walk in your wisdom and truth. I choose to do so, and I ask you to always give me your wisdom in every situation of my life. I praise you for making me free through your truth. In Jesus' name I pray, Amen.

7

KNOWING GOD THROUGH HIS PEACE AND STRENGTH

*For thus saith the Lord God, the Holy One
of Israel; in returning and rest shall ye be
saved; in quietness and in confidence
shall be your strength.*
(Isa. 30:15)

Jesus Is Our Peace, and God Is Our Strength

Jesus is called the Prince of Peace. (See Isa. 9:6.) To His disciples, Jesus said, "Peace I leave with you, my peace I give unto you; not as the world giveth, give I unto you. Let not your heart be troubled, neither let it be afraid" (John 14:27). Much of the feeling of separation from God that we may experience – the distance, the detachment, the disinterestedness – whether conscious or subconscious, is the product of our fears, anxieties, doubts, and a general lack of peace. At such times we need to remember that Jesus came to give us peace.

The angels, in announcing the birth of Jesus Christ to the shepherds, began, "Fear not," and they ended their proclamation with, "Glory to God in the highest, and on earth peace, good will toward men." (See Luke 2:10-14.) The opening admonition is typical of the first words of so many messages from God – we are commanded not to fear.

Perhaps today God would say to us, "*I want to fellowship with you. I want to be a Father to you. I want you to know that I feel goodwill toward you. I want to be your peace and your strength.*"

David wrote, "God is our refuge and strength, a very present help in trouble" (Ps. 46:1). Paul wrote, "I can do all things through Christ which strengtheneth me" (Phil. 4:13).

As we quiet our hearts, and meditate upon His promises, His faithfulness, His mercy, His love, His goodness, and all the qualities of God's character that His Word reveals about Him, faith comes, and confidence arises in our hearts. The confidence we find in Him gives us strength — it is a confidence that is based on the fact that He is able to do what we cannot do, and He is able to be what we cannot be. It is for these reasons that Isaiah wrote, "In quietness and in confidence shall be your strength" (Isa. 30:15).

Paul wrote, "Be careful [anxious] for nothing; but in every thing by prayer and supplication with thanksgiving let your requests be made known unto God. And the peace of God, which passeth all understanding, shall keep your hearts and minds through Christ Jesus" (Phil. 4:6).

A friend of ours had a son who was born with a heart defect that required surgery when the boy was five years old. The father of this boy reported that all of the worries and anxieties of his life paled to insignificance in light of the overwhelming concern he had as his little son faced open-heart surgery.

He said, "Worry about paying the family bills and other concerns of daily life meant nothing to me then. All I cared about was my son and his health. My wife and I took this care to God, and throughout the four-hour operation we experienced a supernatural peace that truly passed all understanding. God was with us, and even though other people expressed their worries to us about our son, we were enveloped in the peace of God."

Our friend's son grew to be a healthy, strong young man who now helps others to find health as a paramedic with an ambulance service. The parents are grateful to God for His peace and His healing touch in their son's life.

The problems of life, as well as the hustle and bustle of the world around us can cause general anxiety in each of our lives, if we let it do so. The Father's antidote for these stresses, as given in the above Scripture, is prayer and supplication, with thanksgiving. When we heed His words about this, we experience a deep, abiding sense of peace that surpasses all understanding. The chaos and confusion may continue to swirl around us, but we are able to enjoy a wonderful peace that stabilizes us and keeps us focused on the One who is our peace and strength.

It is important to note that the thanksgiving aspect of prayer is absolutely crucial to knowing and experiencing God's peace. Through thanksgiving, we acknowledge God's goodness, and this reminds us of the abundant blessings we have received from His hands. This causes joy to spring up within us, and we discover that truly ". . .the joy of the Lord is your strength" (Neh. 8:10).

Joy is such a powerful force in our lives. The Scriptures tell us: "Looking unto Jesus the author and finisher of our faith; who for the joy that was set before him endured the cross, despising the shame, and is set down at the right hand of the throne of God" (Heb. 12:2).

What was the joy that enabled Jesus to endure the cross and despise its shame? It was *you*! He saw you, not just as being redeemed from the curse of death and given eternal life, but completely whole – body, mind, will, emotions, spirit – the whole you!

He saw you tapping into the abundant life He came to give you here and now. He saw you reconciled with the Father and fellowshipping with Him, drinking from the very depths of the wellspring of His love – tasting and seeing that the Lord is good! Those are all wonderful thoughts of joy – the joy that Jesus experienced as He faced the cross.

He saw you as being, "Strengthened with all might, according to his glorious power, unto all patience and longsuffering with joyfulness" (Col. 1:11). As you think about this, let His joy overflow to you. He wants you to know His joy, experience His joy, and share His joy. As you do so, strength is imparted to you.

A Letter From the Father to You

My beloved child, I will keep you in perfect peace if you will trust Me and keep your mind focused on Me.[1] When your ways please Me, I promise to make even your enemies be at peace with you.[2] Love the truth and peace.[3]

You have found peace with Me through Jesus.[4] Always remember that I am not the author of confusion, but of peace.[5] Let My peace rule in your heart.[6] My Son, Jesus, is your peace. It is He who broke down the wall of partition that had once separated Me from you.[7] Because of His obedience, I have ordained peace for you.[8]

It is My delight to give strength to you.[9] I promise to bless you with peace.[10] Jesus gave you His peace, and because of this you no longer need to fear.[11] Do not be anxious, My child. As you come to Me in prayer and supplication with thanksgiving, I promise to give you a supernatural peace that surpasses all understanding. Remember that My peace will keep your heart and mind through Christ Jesus.[12] My beloved child, never forget that I am your strength and song.[13] Remember that My joy is your strength.[14] Because you know Me, you will be strong.[15] It is not by might, nor by power that you shall prevail, but it is by My Spirit, dear child.[16] My strength is made perfect in your weakness.[17] I will strengthen you according to My Word.[18]

Come to Me, and I will grant you, according to the riches of My glory, to be strengthened

with might by My Spirit in your inner self so
that Christ will dwell in your heart by faith and
you will be rooted and grounded in love.[19]

References: *(1) Isaiah 26:3; (2) Proverbs 16:7; (3)
Zechariah 8:19; (4) Romans 5:1; (5) 1 Corinthians 14:33;
(6) Colossians 3:15; (7) Ephesians 2:14; (8) Isaiah 26:12;
(9) Psalms 29:11; (10) John 14:27; (11) John 14:1; (12)
Philippians 4:6-7; (13) Exodus 15:2; (14) Nehemiah 8:10;
(15) Daniel 11:32; (16) Zechariah 4:6; (17) 2 Corinthians
12:9; (18) Psalms 119:28; (19) Ephesians 3:16-17.*

Know God – Know Peace

There is a bumper sticker with a poignant
message that says, "No God – No Peace.
Know God – Know Peace." This play on
words shows us the direct relationship
between knowing God and having peace in
our lives. In fact, the Bible says, "Thou wilt
keep him in perfect peace, whose mind is
stayed on thee: because he trusteth in thee"
(Isa. 26:3).

Our Father is the God of peace, as Paul
proclaims, "And the God of peace shall bruise
Satan under your feet shortly. The grace of
our Lord Jesus Christ be with you. Amen"
(Rom. 16:20). He is the God of peace, and
Jesus is our peace. Through Jesus Christ we
are able to live and walk in peace at all times,
because ". . .in Christ Jesus ye who sometimes
were far off are made nigh by the blood of
Christ. For he is our peace, who hath made

both one, and hath broken down the middle wall of partition between us" (Eph. 2:13-14).

Through the blood of Jesus, therefore, we are able to have access to God, our Father, and this results in our experience of His peace. "Therefore being justified by faith, we have peace with God through our Lord Jesus Christ" (Rom. 5:1). We have peace through Christ, with God, and it is a lasting, deep inner peace that no storm of life can threaten.

An unfaltering trust in God will give us an inner calm regardless of the storm raging around us. It will give us peace in a troubled world torn by strife and hatred, and man's inhumanity to man. It will also give you strength to face whatever storms may come your way.

No Anxiety

As we've noted in the introduction to this chapter, Paul admonishes us to pray with thanksgiving and to let our requests be made known unto God: "Be careful for nothing; but in every thing by prayer and supplication with thanksgiving let your requests be made known unto God. And the peace of God, which passeth all understanding, shall keep your hearts and minds through Christ Jesus" (Phil. 4:6-7).

This is the apostle's prescription for anxiety. In an age of great anxiety, fear, and panic, we can know peace, and the way to know peace is to know God. The peace He gives to us surpasses all understanding.

Jesus said, "Peace I leave with you, my peace I give unto you: not as the world giveth, give I unto you. Let not your heart be troubled, neither let it be afraid" (John 14:27). The world cannot replicate the kind of peace that Jesus gives to us. It is only through Him that we can know true peace in our lives, and nothing in all the world can ever remove such wonderful peace from us.

There need never be any anxiety in a believer's life, because we know the Father is always taking care of us. God cares. Jesus said, "Come to Me, all you who labor and are heavy laden, and I will give you rest" (Matt. 11:28, NKJV). This is an invitation that is far too great to ever refuse.

Yet, it goes without saying it is a peace that we often struggle to access. That is why the Word tells us we must cease from our own labor to enter into God's rest. (See Heb. 4:9-11.) Clearly, unbelief regarding God's Word, doubting His faithfulness and ability, and questioning His desire to care for us in every way keeps us from His rest. Apart from His rest, we will not come to know Him well.

The Father's Will – Our Resting Place

We can rest in the will of God. The acceptance of His will always brings peace to us. Dante, a great Christian writer of the Middle Ages wrote, "In His will is our peace." Where God is, there is peace, because our God is peace. In His presence there is peace. Walking with Him is peace. Knowing His love is peace. Peace is one of the Father's greatest desires for us.

Paul wrote, "To be spiritually minded is life and peace" (Rom. 8:6). To be spiritually minded is to be in tune with God and His will. He has made it possible for us to find rest and peace through Jesus Christ. "In Him we have redemption through His blood, the forgiveness of sins, according to the riches of His grace which He made to abound toward us in all wisdom and prudence, having made known to us the mystery of His will, according to His good pleasure which He purposed in Himself" (Eph. 1:7-9, NKJV).

As we give attention to God's Word and the things of the Spirit (See Rom. 8:5-6.), we become spiritually minded, and this enables us to discern the will of God. Spiritual mindedness really is seeing things – everything – from our Father's perspective. This always results in great personal peace, because we know that we are walking according to God's plan and purpose for our lives.

Jehovah-Shalom

God revealed many of His greatest attributes to the Israelites when they worshiped and honored Him in the face of trouble. For example, when the Israelites were being tormented by the Midianites, Gideon began to seek God. He, and all the men in his army, were afraid. God sent one of His angels to him, and Gideon, a former farmboy who was now in charge of an army, grew even more frightened. He said, "Alas, O Lord God! For I have seen the Angel of the Lord face to face" (Judg. 6:22, NKJV).

God answered Him with gentleness: "Peace be with you; do not fear, you shall not die" (Judg. 6:23, NKJV). What a sweet and comforting message from the Father's heart this was. It was this wonderful experience that led Gideon to erect an altar in honor of Jehovah-Shalom – the Lord Is Our Peace. (See Judg. 6:24.)

God was peace to them in the midst of horrible violence, bloodshed, and war, just as He is to each of us who chooses to honor

Him, worship Him, and praise Him, as Gideon and the Israelites did. He wants to be Jehovah-Shalom to us.

Fortified by peace, Gideon went forth with an army of 32,000 men. However, many of these soldiers were weak and vacillating, so at God's direction Gideon fired all but 300. Knowing that the God-who-is-our-peace was with him enabled Gideon and a mere 300 valiant warriors to subdue the Midianites. "Thus Midian was subdued before the children of Israel, so that they lifted their heads no more. And the country was quiet for forty years in the days of Gideon" (Judg. 8:28, NKJV). Forty years of peace for an entire nation stemmed from the spiritual peace that God gave to His willing, obedient servant.

To have God's peace ruling in our hearts we must have *Him* ruling in our hearts, for he is Jehovah-Shalom. Thomas a Kempis, in his book *The Imitation of Christ*, shares this revelation from the heart of the Father: "If you will hear Me and follow My voice, you shall enjoy much peace. . . .In giving yourself over with all your heart to the divine will, not seeking your own things, either great or small, either in time or in eternity. So shall you keep an even countenance, in thanksgiving, amid prosperity and adversity, weighing all things with an equal balance. . . .

know that you shall then enjoy abundance of peace, as great as your state of sojourning is able to possess."

God Protects Us

God is our strength, and He is our protection as well. The Psalmist wrote a stirring hymn of praise to God, our strength – Psalm 27: "The Lord is my light and my salvation; whom shall I fear? The Lord is the strength of my life; of whom shall I be afraid" (Ps. 27:1).

Because we know God, who is our light and our salvation, we have nothing at all to fear. Because we know Him as the strength of our life, we need never be afraid of anything. Indeed, fear is the opposite of faith, and we are called to be a people of faith. It is a principle of the Kingdom that as we choose to believe God's Word and trust Him, He moves to protect and help us.

The Psalmist continues, "Though an host should encamp against me, my heart shall not fear: though war should rise against me, in this will I be confident" (Ps. 27:3). Even in the midst of battle, there is no reason to fear, because God is our strength, and He is our Protector.

"One thing have I desired of the Lord, that will I seek after; that I may dwell in the house of the Lord all the days of my life, to behold the beauty of the Lord, and to inquire in his temple" (Ps. 27:4). The Psalmist has his priorities in their right order. The most important thing in his life was to seek God and to know Him. His desire was accomplished as he dwelt in the house of God, beholding His beauty, asking Him questions, and receiving His answers. What a great example for each of us to follow!

"For in the time of trouble he shall hide me in his pavilion: in the secret of his tabernacle shall he hide me; he shall set me up upon a rock" (Ps. 27:5). God will hide us in the time of trouble, and he will set us upon a rock – the solid rock of the Lord Jesus Christ and His Word.

"And now shall mine head be lifted up above mine enemies round about me: therefore will I offer in his tabernacle sacrifices of joy; I will sing, yea, I will sing praises unto the Lord" (Ps. 27:6). When God lifts us up above our enemies, surely we have cause to rejoice and sing His praises.

"When my father and my mother forsake, me, then the Lord will take me up" (Ps. 27:10). God will never forsake us, even when family and friends do.

"Teach me thy way, O Lord, and lead me in a plain path, because of mine enemies" (Ps.

27:11). As we get to know God, He teaches us His ways, and He leads us clearly and plainly.

"Wait on the Lord: be of good courage, and he shall strengthen thine heart: wait, I say, on the Lord" (Ps. 27:14). Strength of heart comes from waiting on God.

Dwight L. Moody wrote, "We are constantly limiting God's power by our own ideas. Let us get our eyes off one another and fix them on God. Nothing is too hard for Him."

The Holy Spirit Is the Strengthener

When we surrender ourselves to the Spirit of God, we will learn more about God's strengthening grace and His all-embracing love in a week, than we would learn in a lifetime, apart from the Spirit.

Our God is omnipotent (all-powerful), and He often reveals His power and strength to us through the Holy Spirit. For example, Paul wrote: "But if the Spirit of him that raised up Jesus from the dead dwell in you, he that raised up Christ from the dead shall also quicken your mortal bodies by his Spirit that dwelleth in you" (Rom. 8:11).

Our bodies are the temple of the Holy Spirit – a sanctuary in which God has chosen to dwell. "What? Know ye not that your body is the temple of the Holy Ghost which is in

you, which ye have of God, and ye are not
your own?" (1 Cor. 6:19).

The power and strength of God live
within us by His Holy Spirit. That is an
amazing truth. The revelation of it releases
spiritual power in our lives which has the
effect of strengthening our body while it
strengthens our spirit. The Greek word
dunamis is often used in reference to the
power of the Holy Spirit which is available to
us. This word is the root word for dynamic,
dynamo, and dynamite. Dynamite power, by
way of the Holy Spirit, enables us to be
dynamic witnesses, more than conquerors
(spiritual dynamos), and stronger people.

"But ye shall receive power, after that the
Holy Ghost is come upon you: and ye shall be
witnesses unto me. . ." (Acts 1:8). This is why
we are commanded to ". . .be filled with the
Spirit" (Eph. 5:18). Many Christians are
experiencing the blessing of being filled
afresh each day with the Holy Spirit. The
word "filled" (in Eph. 5:18) actually implies
that we are to be receiving a continuous
infilling, one that never stops. The Holy Spirit
wants to flow like a river within our hearts.
(See John 7:38.)

Paul writes, "For our gospel came not
unto you in word only, but also in power, and
in the Holy Ghost, and in much assurance; as

ye know what manner of men we were among you for your sake" (1 Thess. 1:5). The power of the Holy Spirit gives us a deep assurance from God, our Father.

The Holy Spirit brings liberty to us, and His power changes us to be more like Jesus. "Now the Lord is that Spirit: and where the Spirit of the Lord is, there is liberty. But we all, with open face beholding as in a glass the glory of the Lord, are changed into the same image from glory to glory, even as by the Spirit of the Lord" (2 Cor. 3:17-18).

When Jesus calls the Holy Spirit "the Comforter," He is actually implying that He is our strength, and His strength is what brings comfort to us. The word "Comforter," as applied to the Holy Spirit, is (in the original Greek) *Paracletos*, which means Helper, Advocate, and Strengthener. Literally, then, the Holy Spirit is the Strengthener. Jesus promised us that "The Strengthener" will be with us forever. This is a powerful promise that inspires us to live victoriously in the strength He provides. (See Eph. 3.)

J.B. Phillips, well-known for the Phillips translation of the Bible, wrote, "Every time we say, 'I believe in the Holy Spirit,' we mean that we believe that there is a living God able and willing to enter human personality and change it."

*The kingdom of God is not in
word, but in power.*
(1 Cor. 4:20)

Prayer Response: Father, thank you for your peace which keeps my heart and mind through Christ. Thank you for your joy which truly is my strength. Thank you for your strength which enables me to do all things through Christ. I choose to walk in your peace, joy, and strength every step of the way. In Jesus' name I pray, Amen.

8

KNOWING GOD AS OUR HEALER AND PROVIDER

He sent his word, and healed them,
and delivered them from their destructions.
(Ps. 107:20)

God's Provision Includes Healing

Healing is a part of God's provision in our lives. Paul wrote, "And my God shall supply all your need according to His riches in glory by Christ Jesus" (Phil. 4:19, NKJV). Inherent in this promise is the truth that if we need healing (or anything else), God will provide it for us.

The distinction between God as Healer and God as Provider is an important one. Indeed, even God makes this distinction in His Word. Two of the names of God are *Jehovah-Jireh* ("the Lord will provide" – Gen. 22:13-14, NKJV) and *Jehovah-Rapha* ("I am the Lord who heals you – Exod. 15:26, NKJV). The scriptural contexts in which these names first appear give us a picture of Jehovah-Jireh providing the sacrificial ram to take Isaac's place on the altar (a foreshadowing of His provision through Jesus for each of us to be spared eternal death); and the name of

Jehovah-Rapha is announced in conjunction with keeping God's commandments in order to let us know that the Lord is our Healer. In both cases, we see a direct connection between our obedience and God being our Healer and our Provider.

The Bible says, "Trust in the Lord with all thine heart; and lean not unto thine own understanding. In all thy ways acknowledge him, and he shall direct thy paths. Be not wise in thine own eyes; fear the Lord, and depart from evil. It shall be health to thy navel, and marrow to thy bones. Honour the Lord with thy substance, and with the firstfruits of all thine increase; So shall thy barns be filled with plenty, and thy presses shall burst out with new wine" (Prov. 3:5-10).

There is, perhaps, no more succinct explanation in the entire Bible of how life in God is supposed to work. We must trust the Lord instead of ourselves. We must acknowledge that He is God – that He created us, knows best how to care for us, and is infinitely wiser than we are – and we must permit Him to direct our paths. Obeying Him, we are able to recognize His rightful sovereignty over our lives and everything we have. As a result, we give back the first fruits of all He blesses us with. As we follow His guidelines, we will experience both God's healing and His provision in our lives. In fact, He will give us good health and prosperity.

It would bankrupt any national government to try to provide feed for every bird in the world for one year. Our heavenly Father, however, manages to do this with no strain at all. (See Matt. 6.) In fact, He knows when a sparrow falls to the ground. (See Matt. 10:29.)

We trust Christ for salvation, but when it comes to trusting Him with all other aspects of our lives, we may find ourselves falling short. Jesus said, "Take no thought for your life, what ye shall eat, or what ye shall drink; nor yet for your body, what ye shall put on. Is not the life more than meat and the body than raiment? Behold the fowls of the air: for they sow not, neither do they reap, nor gather into barns, yet your heavenly Father feedeth them. Are ye not much better than they? . . .But seek ye first the kingdom of God, and his righteousness, and all these things shall be added unto you" (Matt. 6:25-26, 33).

As you examine God's promises in this chapter concerning His faithful provision, including healing, may your faith blossom in such a way that you will learn to walk in the fullness of God's provision in every area of your life.

A Letter From the Father to You

Beloved, I wish above all things that you would prosper and be in health, even as your soul prospers.[1] By Jesus' stripes you are able to receive healing, My child.[2] Remember that Jesus, the Great Physician, is the same yesterday, and today, and forever.[3] He forgives all your iniquities, and heals all your diseases.[4]

Ask Me for healing, and I will heal you.[5] I will restore health to you, and I will heal you of all wounds,[6] for I am your God, I am your Healer.[7]

My child, I promise always to deal well with you, according to My Word.[8] Behold, I am with you, and I will keep you wherever you go. I will not leave you. I will do what I've promised to you.[9] Indeed, I promise to supply all of your needs according to My riches in glory, through Christ Jesus.[10]

Dearly beloved, seek first My kingdom and My righteousness, and all the things you are concerned about will be taken care of.[11] Remember that I will make all things work together for good in your life because you love Me and are called according to My purpose.[12]

Call unto Me, and I will answer you.[13]

References: (1) 3 John 2; (2) Isaiah 53:5; (3) Hebrews 13:8; (4) Psalms 103:3; (5) Jeremiah

17:14; (6) *Jeremiah 30:17;* (7) *Exodus 15:26;* (8) *Psalms 119:65;* (9) *Genesis 28:15;* (10) *Philippians 4:19;* (11) *Matthew 6:33;* (12) *Romans 8:28;* (13) *Jeremiah 33:3.*

The Lord Who Heals Us

God is the Healer of our souls and bodies. He is *Jehovah-Rapha,* the Lord who heals us. "If thou wilt diligently hearken to the voice of the Lord thy God, and wilt do that which is right in his sight, and wilt give ear to his commandments, and keep all his statutes, I will put none of these diseases upon thee, which I have brought upon the Egyptians: for I am the Lord that healeth thee" (Exod. 15:25-26).

This passage shows us that God wants us to know Him as our Healer. Notice, however, that the first step in receiving healing from our Father is to be in an obedient relationship with Him. Here we have both a commandment to obey, and a promise to claim. It is important to realize that both are interconnected.

Acknowledging God as our Father, and learning to obey Him are important steps in knowing Him as our Healer. Likewise, trusting God must be in place. Then we will be able to agree with the truth expressed by Jeremiah in behalf of God: "For I know the thoughts that I think toward you, saith the

Lord, thoughts of peace, and not of evil, to give you an expected end. Then shall ye call upon me, and ye shall go and pray unto me, and I will hearken unto you. And ye shall seek me, and find me, when ye shall search for me with all your heart" (Jer. 29:11-13).

God thinks thoughts of peace toward us, and He also thinks thoughts of healing, as John divulges: "Beloved, I pray that you may prosper in all things and be in health, just as your soul prospers" (3 John 2, NKJV).

When sickness comes to God's people, we can know Him as our Healer.

Andrew Murray wrote, "When I bring my sickness to the Lord, I do not depend on what I see, what I feel, or what I think, but on what He says. Even when everything appears contrary to the expected healing, even if it should not take place at the time or in the way that I had thought I should receive it, even when the symptoms seem only to be aggravated, my faith, strengthened by the very waiting, should cling immovably to this word which has gone out of the mouth of God: 'I am the Lord that healeth thee.'"

A minister in the Church of the Brethren, an Anabaptist denomination, with its roots in the German Reformation, underwent brain scans as a result of certain physical problems he was experiencing. The brain scans revealed a large mass within his brain.

He was sent by his local physician to a group of specialists at a university hospital. They all examined him, gave him additional tests, and determined that brain surgery would be required in the very near future.

The pastor went home, and asked his family and congregation to pray for him. He called for the elders to come and anoint him with oil, in accord with James 5:14: "Is anyone among you sick? Let him call for the elders of the church, and let them pray over him, anointing him with oil in the name of the Lord" (James 5:14, NKJV). This is a doctrine that is devotedly adhered to by the Brethren.

The teaching also includes this promise: "And the prayer of faith will save the sick, and the Lord will raise him up" (James 5:15, NKJV).

The elders, the congregation, the pastor's family, and the pastor himself claimed this promise for his healing. When he returned to the university hospital, the surgeons ordered another pre-op brain scan, only to discover that the mass they had all seen before could no longer be found!

They all exclaimed, "We don't know what happened! We saw it with our own eyes! This is incredible!" Then they told the pastor, "Surgery is no longer required," and he went home to continue his ministry to his congregation and his family.

This is only one example among countless others that He is the same yesterday, today, and forever, and that He wants us to know Him as our Healer.

We Are Healed Through the Stripes of Jesus

Prophesying of Jesus, Isaiah wrote, "He is despised and rejected by men, a Man of sorrows and acquainted with grief. And we hid, as it were, our faces from Him; He was despised, and we did not esteem Him. Surely He has borne our griefs [sicknesses] and carried our sorrows; yet we esteemed Him stricken, smitten by God, and afflicted. But He was wounded for our transgressions, He was bruised for our iniquities; the chastisement for our peace was upon Him, and by His stripes we are healed" (Isa. 53:3-5, NKJV).

In the same way that we receive salvation through the blood of Jesus, we receive healing by His stripes as well. The above verse from Isaiah is referred to by Matthew as he is describing one of the healings performed by

Jesus: "When evening had come, they brought to Him many who were demon-possessed. And He cast out the spirits with a word, and healed all who were sick, that it might be fulfilled which was spoken by Isaiah the prophet, saying: 'He Himself took our infirmities and bore our sicknesses'" (Matt. 8:16-17, NKJV).

This concept is reiterated to the New Testament Church by the Apostle Peter: "Who his own self bare our sins in his own body on the tree, that we, being dead to sins, should live unto righteousness: by whose stripes ye were healed" (1 Pet. 2:24).

These Scriptures, along with James 5:14-16, lead us to an understanding of God's great mercy expressed through Christ's passion and His redemptive work on the cross.

What does this teach us about the Father? It shows us that He cares about every aspect of our lives, including our physical condition. He does not want us to be ill, and He has provided a way for us to find healing through Christ. The redemptive work of our Savior includes healing for the whole person – spirit, soul, and body.

When a sick child goes to his father or mother seeking help and comfort, the parent responds with love and compassion. The immediate response of the father or mother is to do everything within his or her power to bring healing to the child. The same is true with our Father in heaven. He wants us to be well, and He has the power to effect healing in our lives.

The Bible says, "So shall you serve the Lord your God, and He will bless your bread and your water. And I will take sickness away from the midst of you" (Exod. 23:25, NKJV).

Healing Promises From the Father to His Children

The Bible presents us with many healing promises. They show us that God always wants the best for us in every area of our lives:

"But to you who fear My name the Sun of Righteousness shall arise with healing in His wings; and you shall go out and grow fat like stall-fed calves. You shall trample the wicked, for they shall be ashes under the soles of your feet on the day that I do this, says the Lord of hosts" (Mal. 4:2-3, NKJV).

"Who forgiveth all thine iniquities; who healeth all thy diseases" (Ps. 103:3).

"He healeth the broken in heart, and bindeth up their wounds" (Ps. 147:3).

"For I will restore health unto thee, and I will heal thee of thy wounds, saith the Lord" (Jer. 30:17).

"And Jesus went about all the cities and villages, teaching in their synagogues, and preaching the gospel of the kingdom, and healing every sickness and every disease among the people" (Matt. 9:35).

"Who his own self bare our sins in his own body on the tree, that we, being dead to sins, should live unto righteousness: by whose stripes ye were healed" (1 Pet. 2:24).

"Heal me, O Lord, and I shall be healed; save me, and I shall be saved: for thou art my praise" (Jer. 17:14).

"My son, attend to my words; incline thine ear unto my sayings. Let them not depart from thine eyes; keep them in the midst of thine heart. For they are life unto those that find them, and health to all their flesh" (Prov. 4:20-22).

These promises emanate from God's heart. They show us how much He loves us and wants to help us. They reveal the truth that He is our Healer.

Andrew Murray wrote, "Place your foot firmly on the immovable rock of God's own Word. Pray to the Lord to manifest His almightiness in your body because you are one of the members of *His* Body, and the temple of the Holy Spirit. Persevere in believing in Him with the firm assurance that He has undertaken for you, that He has made Himself responsible for your body, and that His healing power will glorify Him in you even as it heals you."

Understanding the Healer

The heart of a good physician is always focused on helping others get well. Such an individual studies medicine in order to know how he might best bring healing to his patients. He listens to their cries and complaints, and he tries to diagnose their problem in an effort to find the best course of treatment to apply to their condition. He even takes a binding commitment – the Hippocratic Oath – which articulates his desire to effect healing in the lives of others.

God, as our Healer, shares these same concerns, but He already knows what the problem is, and He knows what must be done in order to effect healing in our lives. Jesus said, "Your Father knows the things you have need of before you ask Him" (Matt. 6:8, NKJV).

Many times God brings healing to people through the important work of physicians. Our family has often benefited from the services of doctors who were committed to the very best care for each of their patients. We thank God for the many times they have helped us.

Our family has also experienced God's healing touch apart from medical intervention. On one occasion a few years ago, Kathleen was facing the possibility of two major operations due to some physical problems she was experiencing. One of these surgeries could have resulted in major complications. After much prayer and consultation with both her pastor and her doctor, Kathleen decided to have one operation, but she strongly felt that the second operation was not God's will for her. We thanked God that the first operation went smoothly with no complications.

Concerning the other condition, we and our Church family as well as our immediate family prayed diligently for her healing, and God heard and answered our prayers. After several months the painful symptoms she had been experiencing were gone, and she was completely healed without medical intervention. Because she felt that she had heard from God that she was not to have the second operation, she stood her ground in faith, and God honored her faith with a complete healing.

God knows what we need, and this realization is the point of trust, faith, and acceptance in our relationship with Him. When we know that "Every good gift and every perfect gift [including healing] is from above, and comes down from the Father of lights, with whom there is no variation or shadow of turning" (James 1:17, NKJV), then we are able to trust our Father for the healing we seek.

Knowing God as Our Provider

The word *providence*, as it relates to God, is frequently used to refer to His divine guidance or care in our lives. When the word is capitalized it refers to God himself, most particularly as the Power that sustains and guides human destiny.

Our Father is our Providence. He cares about us, and He wants to help us meet every need. He is *Jehovah-Jireh*, God our Provider. It has been said quite accurately that Providence knows what we need better than we ourselves. This is a vivid description of our Father in heaven.

Jesus said, "Your Father knows the things you have need of before you ask Him" (Matt. 6:8, NKJV). Then, in outline fashion, the Master went on to spell out the correct form of prayer: "In this manner, therefore, pray:

Our Father in heaven, hallowed be Your name. Your kingdom come. Your will be done on earth as it is in heaven. *Give us this day our daily bread.* And forgive us our debts, as we forgive our debtors. And do not lead us into temptation, but deliver us from the evil one. For Yours is the kingdom and the power and the glory forever. Amen" (Matt. 6:9-13, NKJV).

In this prayer, commonly called the Lord's Prayer, we find the key components of prayer: Adoration, confession, thanksgiving, and supplication. The supplication part of prayer ("Give us this day our daily bread" – Matt. 6:11, NKJV) asks God to supply our needs. A supplicant is one who goes before an authority figure and requests that a need be met or a situation be taken care of. Supplication, therefore, is a humble and earnest entreaty to the providence of God.

Jesus' model prayer is supplicatory in that it asks God to meet all of our needs – physical and spiritual – and Jesus' intimate relationship with the Father assures us that God will hear and answer our prayers. He said, "Most assuredly, I say to you, whatever you ask the Father in My name He will give you" (John 16:23, NKJV).

When God supplied the need of Abraham by way of a sacrificial ram atop Mount

Moriah just before he had prepared to sacrifice his only son, Isaac, as a burnt offering, He became Jehovah-jireh for all of us. "And Abraham called the name of the place, The-Lord-Will-Provide; as it is said to this day" (Gen. 22:14, NKJV).

God's provision in our lives is seen moment by moment, and day by day, because He is our faithful Father who knows what we need and always wants to help us meet our needs.

An Italian peasant who lived on top of a mountain, at least a mile away from his nearest neighbor, was asked how he could live alone in a small cottage high in the mountains. His answer was simple and direct: "Providence is my next-door neighbor." This is the proper attitude of every child of God.

Jesus said, "Therefore I say to you, whatever things you ask when you pray, believe that you receive them, and you will have them" (Mark 11:24, NKJV).

Our Greatest Need

The greatest need of our life is to know God intimately. When this need is met, all other needs are met as well. Jesus said, "But seek first the kingdom of God and His righteousness, and all these things shall be added to you" (Matt. 6:33, NKJV). The famous missionary Hudson Taylor once remarked, "God's work done in God's way cannot fail to have God's provision."

Certainly this was proven true by men like George Mueller who operated a Christian orphanage in Bristol, England. Mueller trusted implicitly in the Providence of God. He truly believed that every need of his orphans would be met, and God always came through for him. Once, when the cupboards were bare, the boys set the dinner table, gathered for dinner, and said their grace. There wasn't a bit of food in the facility, but George Mueller believed that God would meet their need.

A knock was heard at the door. It was a railroad man who announced that a train carrying an abundance of food had just derailed. Realizing that the food would soon spoil, he offered it to the headmaster. Voila! Dinner was served.

That is God's faithful providence, and it is also Mueller's faithful trust in God's providence displayed for all to see. "But without faith it is impossible to please Him, for he who comes to God must believe that

He is, and that He is a rewarder of those who diligently seek Him" (Heb. 11:6, NKJV).

God's All-Sufficient Grace

Paul gives us a clear picture of God's all-sufficient grace at work in our lives: "And God is able to make all grace abound toward you; that ye, always having all sufficiency in all things, may abound to every good work" (2 Cor. 9:8). This is abounding grace, and it is the Father's faithful providence at work.

The Psalmist describes God's grace for us as well: "For thou, Lord, wilt bless the righteous; with favour wilt thou compass him as with a shield" (Ps. 5:12). God's grace is His loving favor in our lives; it is experienced in the blessings He bestows upon us.

Jonathan Edwards, the father of the Great Awakening in colonial America, wrote, "God's providence may be compared to a large and long river with innumerable branches beginning in different regions and at a great distance from each other. They continue for a while in their varied and contrary courses, yet the nearer they approach their common end, the more they gather together. At last they all discharge themselves at one mouth into the same ocean. To us the many streams of this river are apt to appear like mere jumble and confusion, because we cannot see from one branch to another and cannot see the whole at once. Yet if we trace each of them, we see that they all unite at last and all empty themselves at one point into the same great ocean. Not one of all the streams fails to arrive there at last. That is what God's providence is like."

God's providence fills a mighty ocean with His love, and it is our privilege, as His children, to enjoy all the blessings that ocean has to offer. As we splash in the surf of God's providence, like little children at the seashore, our cares evaporate in the sunshine of God's love, and we are showered with His blessings.

Providence stems from the grace of our faithful God who promises to make known to us ". . .the mystery of his will according to his good pleasure" (Eph. 1:9). God pours out His grace upon us. He meets every need of our lives.

Alexander Maclaren, a Christian writer, sums up the qualities of God's providence and provision in our lives by saying: "Get near to God if you want to enjoy what He has prepared for you. Live in simple, loving fellowship with Him if you desire to drink in His fullness. . . .If we want to get our needs supplied, our weakness strengthened, and wisdom to dispel our perplexity, we must be where all the provision is stored. . . .If we will not ascend the hill of the Lord and stand in His holy place by simple faith, God's amplest provision will be nothing to us, and we will be empty in the middle of affluence."

> *Surely goodness and mercy shall follow*
> *me all the days of my life; and*
> *I will dwell in the house of*
> *the Lord forever.*
> (Ps. 23:6, NKJV)

Prayer Response: Dear Father-God, thank you for being both my Healer and my Provider. Truly, you do supply all of my needs according to your riches in glory, including physical, financial, emotional, spiritual, and vocational needs. Thank you for meeting my needs and giving me hope. In Jesus' name I pray, Amen.

PART III

AVENUES TO INTIMACY

PART III

AVENUES TO INTIMACY

An avenue is a thoroughfare which enables us to go from one location to another. Synonyms for "avenue" include way, street, road, bypass, highway, and route. As Christians, we are pilgrims and wayfarers who are traveling along life's way in order to get closer to God. He is our destination, and intimacy with Him is our goal. There are several routes for us to follow in order to know our Father intimately.

In the following section of *Knowing God Intimately* you will discover that the avenues to intimacy with God include His Word, His creation, His presence, faith, obedience, prayer, fellowship, praise, and worship.

God's Word gives us light as we travel through this darkened world. The presence of God guides us and cheers us along the way. We walk by faith and obedience, not by sight. Prayer, praise, and worship are the avenues that lead us to the very throne-room of God where we are able to have fellowship with our Father.

It is interesting to note that even while this book was being prepared, neurologists were unveiling evidence from a new field known as "neurotheology" to suggest that our brains are "hard-wired" for spiritual experience in the same way that they are "hard-wired" for language acquisition and motor development.

These scientists have discovered what seem to be "spiritual circuits" in the brain which become very active and responsive when one is involved in prayer, contemplation, worship, and meditation. To the believer, such research will seem elementary and redundant when he knows these truths through personal experience with God.

It is not surprising that these discoveries are being made. God created us to have fellowship with Him through prayer, worship, praise, thanksgiving, nature, and the various other avenues we discuss in this section. He has provided us with several means of connecting with Him. Each is wonderful and exciting.

As you read the following section we urge you to follow each of these means and avenues to intimacy with God. As you do so, He will become more real to you than He ever has been before.

9

KNOWING GOD THROUGH HIS WORD

*For the word of God is living and powerful,
and sharper than any two-edged sword,
piercing even to the division of soul
and spirit, . . .and is a discerner of the
thoughts and intents of the heart.*
(Heb. 4:12, NKJV)

The Living Word

Bible scholars tell us that there is a difference between the Word of God as *logos* (the written Word contained in the Bible), and *rhema* (the Word becoming a living, specific reality governing our lives). These are vitally important concepts for us to understand as we take a look at the Word of God being an avenue to *Knowing God Intimately*.

We can read the Bible from cover to cover every year of our lives. We can even memorize portions of it, as many have done, but if all this remains in the realm of "head knowledge," as opposed to "heart knowledge," we will not know God any better than we did at the outset.

However, when we begin to hear the Word as if God, the Father, were speaking directly and personally to us, perhaps concerning the problem we are facing or our next important decision, it becomes a Living Word.

It is impossible to overemphasize the importance of the Word of God to us. It is absolutely central to *Knowing God Intimately*. It is where our personal journey begins, and where it ends.

A Letter From the Father to You

My lovely child, you are so special to Me.[1] For this reason, I've established an eternal covenant with you.[2] The promises of My Word will never fail you.[3] Please take your stand upon My promises.[4]

Study My Word so that you will never need to be ashamed.[5] The Bible is fully inspired by My Holy Spirit, and it is profitable to you in so many ways.[6] My Word is powerful and it is alive. In fact, it is sharper than any sword. Let its truth pierce deep within you. As it does so, it will divide your soul from your spirit, and it will discern the thoughts and intents of your heart.[7]

I promise you that My Word will never return unto Me void. It always will accomplish those things that I desire, and it will prosper in every way wherever I send it.[8] Search the Scriptures, my child, for in them you will find eternal life, and you will learn more about Me and My ways.[9]

My Word is settled in heaven.[10] All of My promises to you are Yes and Amen in Christ Jesus.[11] Never forget that I've given you exceeding great and precious promises, and through My promises you will be able to partake of My very nature, as you escape the corruption that is in the world through lust.[12]

Let My Word be a lamp unto your feet, and a light unto your path as you continue your journey through a darkened world.[13] As you go, My Word will lead you. When you sleep, My Word will keep you. When you awaken, I will talk with you through My Word.[14] I will instruct you and teach you in the way which you should take, and I will guide you with My eye.[15] My child, I will restore your soul, and I will lead you in the paths of righteousness for My name's sake because I love you.[16]

Do not let My Word depart from your mouth. Meditate upon My Word day and night, and observe to do all that is written within it. As you do these things, you will soon discover that I will bless you with prosperity and the greatest possible success.[17]

My Word imparts faith to your heart, dear child.[18] As you receive that faith and act upon it, I am greatly pleased.[19] Nothing is impossible with Me, dear child.[20]

References: (1) Song of Solomon 7:10; (2) 2 Peter 1:4-8; (3) 2 Peter 3:9; (4) John 14:14; (5) 2 Timothy 2:15; (6) 2 Timothy 3:16-17; (7) Hebrews 4:12; (8) Isaiah 55:10-11; (9) Acts 17:11; (10) Psalms 119:89; (11) 2 Corinthians 1:20; (12) 2 Peter 1:4; (13) Psalms 119:105; (14) Proverbs 6:22-23; (15) Psalms 32:8; (16) Psalms 23:3; (17) Joshua 1:8; (18) Romans 10:17; (19) Hebrews 11:6; (20) Luke 1:37.

Increasing in the Knowledge of God

Paul's prayer for the Colossians reveals the major importance of increasing in the knowledge of God. He prayed: "That ye might walk worthy of the Lord unto all pleasing, being fruitful in every good work, and *increasing in the knowledge of God*; strengthened with all might, according to his glorious power, unto all patience and longsuffering with joyfulness; giving thanks unto the Father, which hath made us meet to be partakers of the inheritance of the saints in light" (Col. 1:10-12).

One vital way to increase in the knowledge of God is through His Word, for the Bible opens the eyes and ears of faith to us: "So then faith comes by hearing, and hearing by the word of God" (Rom. 10:17, NKJV).

The Bible leads us into the very heart of God. The more we immerse ourselves in its truths, the more we get to know its Author. Every author who writes a book inserts something of his or her own life into its writing – something, perhaps, from the author's personal experience, interests, values, and beliefs. The same is true with the Holy Bible which was written by our God.

"All Scripture is given by inspiration of God, and is profitable for doctrine, for reproof, for correction, for instruction in righteousness, that the man of God may be complete, thoroughly equipped for every good work" (2 Tim. 3:16, NKJV).

People of the Book

People of God are people of the Book. As William Evans points out, "The Bible is not merely *a* book, however. It is the Book – the Book that from the importance of its subjects, the wideness of its range, the majesty of its Author, stands as high above all other books as the heaven is high above the earth."

The Bible is our compass, our road map, our manual, and our mirror. It is also a self-portrait of its author, designed to show us who He is so that we can get to know Him and become more like Him.

Through the Word of God we learn several things about our heavenly Father:

> *He is militant. (See Exod. 15:3.)*
> *He is glorious in holiness.*
>   *(See Exod. 15:11.)*
> *He is merciful. (See Exod. 34:6.)*
> *He is a consuming fire. (See Deut. 4:24.)*
> *He is a God of truth. (See Deut. 32:4.)*
> *He is righteous. (See 2 Chron. 12:6.)*
> *He is good. (See Ps. 100:5.)*
> *He is gracious. (See Ps. 145:8.)*
> *He is forgiving. (See Dan. 9:9.)*
> *He is faithful. (See 1 Cor. 1:9.)*
> *He is the God of all comfort.*
>   *(See 2 Cor. 1:3.)*

God's Words Speak Life to Us

It is said that a good novelist will be sure to let dialogue between the characters take up at least a third of the novel. Dialogue is important because it enables the reader to get to know the characters – their thoughts, feelings, beliefs, and attitudes. Through the characters' words, therefore, we get to know what is going on inside of them.

The same is true with God. Through His words we get to know His heart. Jesus said,

"The words that I speak to you are spirit, and they are life" (John 6:63, NKJV). By revealing His heart to us through His Word, God is able to help us understand His person and His purposes, and this makes our life so much fuller and richer.

God's Word actually commands us to know Him. "Know thou the God of thy father" (1 Chron. 28:9).

The Psalmist writes the following words in behalf of God: "Be still, and know that I am God" (Ps. 46:10). God wants us to know Him, and He has given us His Word to enable us to understand Him and His ways.

One definition of a Christian disciple is a person whose life is under the Lordship and direction of Jesus Christ. We learn what the Lord expects of us by reading His Word. That's why we read our Bibles daily, so that we will receive God's direction for our lives. This practice gives us access to all the treasures of God's wisdom and knowledge and helps to keep us on the right track. Diligently seeking God through His Word helps to keep our hearts in tune to hear His voice and receive His direction for our lives.

How sweet are thy words unto my taste!
Yea, sweeter than honey to my mouth!
Through thy precepts I get understanding:
therefore I hate every false way.
Thy word is a lamp unto my feet,
and a light unto my path.
(Ps. 119:103-105)

Prayer Response: Heavenly Father, thank you for your Word which is a lamp unto my feet and a light unto my path. Enable me to walk in the light your Word provides for me each day. I rejoice in the living, dynamic power of your Word, and I will keep on studying it, sharing it, meditating upon it, living it, memorizing it, and letting it renew my mind throughout my life. In Jesus' name I pray, Amen.

10

KNOWING GOD THROUGH FAITH AND OBEDIENCE

But without faith it is impossible to
please Him, for he who comes to
God must believe that He is, and
that He is a rewarder of those
who diligently seek Him.
(Heb. 11:6, NKJV)

Obedient Faith

Take a moment to let the full impact of the above verse from the Bible get past your head and sink into your spirit. Without faith, it is impossible to please God! No matter how much I give of myself, no matter what wonderful things I may do in His name, it is not possible for me to please Him, unless I am operating in faith.

What does it mean to operate in faith? First, obviously, we must believe that God is. And believing "that He is," is not an act of intellectual assent. It is a spirit-level realization, not only that He is, but who He is. It is He who created us. It is he who sustains life in and for us. And it is He, and He alone, who authored the purpose for each life and is able to bring that purpose to pass.

Jesus said, ". . .without me ye can do nothing" (John 15:5). One person shared, "I used to wonder how that could be true, since every day, before I knew Him as my Savior, I got up, fed myself, went to work, provided for my family, and did many, many things without Him. Then I came to realize that, apart from God, nothing has eternal life or value. So, everything I do apart from Him – apart from faith in Him – is nothing. It is without eternal life and without eternal value and, at some point, will be consumed away as stubble by a fire." That is why Paul says, "For whatsoever is not of faith is sin" (Rom. 14:23). Or, as John puts it, "All unrighteousness is sin" (1 John 5:17).

Next, we must believe our righteousness is in Christ. We have none of our own and there is no way we can earn it. It is established in our lives as we grow in Him and obey Him. "If we confess our sins, he is faithful and just to forgive us our sins, and to cleanse us from all unrighteousness" (1 John 1:9). That is how the believer maintains righteousness; there is no other way. Cleansing comes by the operation of faith, accepting God's Word as true and acting upon it.

According to Hebrews 11:6, it is faith which brings God's love and blessings to us.

We find God and we experience His rewards by seeking Him diligently through faith and obeying Him in love. When we find Him, we will realize that fellowship with Him is its own reward. We will fall in love with Him and trust in Him completely.

In the following pages, we will learn a great deal more from God's Word about faith and obedience. But, everything else about faith and obedience will be far more meaningful once we have seen how crucial they are to pleasing the God we desire to know.

A Letter From the Father to You

My beloved child, your faith pleases Me.[1] To build your faith, always listen to My Word.[2] Always remember that I am more than able to perform everything that I've promised to you.[3] Beloved, build yourself up on your most holy faith, praying in the Holy Spirit, and always be sure to keep yourself in My love as you look for the mercy of your Lord Jesus Christ.[4]

Never forget that you walk by faith, not by sight.[5] All things are possible when you truly believe.[6] I am your God. Is anything too hard for Me?[7] Remember that the measure of faith you have comes from Me,[8] and Jesus is the Author and Finisher of your faith. Never forget that He endured the cross for you, and now He is sitting at My right hand.[9]

How it pleases Me, dear one, to know that you love Me even though you have not seen Me. Through faith you are able to rejoice with unspeakable joy that is filled with glory. This enables you to receive the end of your faith, even the salvation of your soul.[10]

I want you always to realize that your faith is the victory that will overcome the world.[11] Your faith determines what will happen in your life.[12] If you will only believe, you will discover that all things are possible to you.[13]

Do not let My Word depart from your mouth.[14] Walk in all My ways.[15] Keep My commandments.[16] Walk before Me in integrity of heart, and in uprightness.[17] Set your heart and your soul to seek Me.[18]

Lay up My words in your heart.[19] My way is strength to you.[20] When you keep My Word you will be happy.[21] Obey My voice, and I will be your God.[22]

References: (1) Hebrews 11:6; (2) Romans 10:17; (3) Romans 4:20-21; (4) Jude 20, 21; (5) 2 Corinthians 5:7; (6) Mark 9:23; (7) Jeremiah 32:27; (8) Romans 12:3; (9) Hebrews 12:2; (10) 1 Peter 1:7-9; (11) 1 John 5:4; (12) Matthew 9:28-29; (13) Mark 9:23; (14) Joshua 1:8; (15) Joshua 22:5; (16) Joshua 22:5; (17) 1 Kings 9:4; (18) 1 Chronicles 22:19; (19) Job 22:22; (20) Proverbs 10:29; (21) Proverbs 29:18; (22) Jeremiah 7:23.

Faith Gives Us Access to the Throne of God

Paul writes, "Therefore, having been justified by faith, we have peace with God through our Lord Jesus Christ, through whom also we have access by faith into this grace in which we stand, and rejoice in hope of the glory of God" (Rom. 5:1-2, NKJV).

It is faith that enables us to see God who is invisible. "While we look not at the things which are seen, but at the things which are not seen: for the things which are seen are temporal; but the things which are not seen are eternal" (2 Cor. 4:18).

Our awesome God is not seen by the naked eye, but faith enables us to know Him, for ". . .we walk by faith, not by sight" (2 Cor. 5:7, NKJV). The sight we receive through faith is spiritual vision that opens our eyes to God as He really is, and this enables us to receive His grace.

Paul writes, "For by grace you have been saved through faith, and that not of yourselves; it is the gift of God, not of works, lest anyone should boast" (Eph. 2:8-9, NKJV).

The grace of God to which we have access through faith is described most poignantly for us by Charles H. Spurgeon: "It is the glory of God's grace that it meets every need of the sinner. If the sinner is dead, it gives him life; if he is filthy, it washes him; if he is naked, it gives him clothing. Is the sinner hungry? It feeds him. Is he thirsty? It gives him something to drink. Do the sinner's needs grow even larger after he becomes a saint, or does he gain a broader perception of them? Then the supplies are just as deep as his need. Bottomless mines are the treasures of divine grace."

An anonymous writer puts it this way: "Faith is the wire that connects you to grace, and over which grace comes streaming from God." Faith is man's response to God's grace.

The truth is, "And my God shall supply all your need according to His riches in glory by Christ Jesus" (Phil. 4:19, NKJV).

Knowing God Is
Believing in Him

Paul wrote to Timothy, "I am not ashamed, for I know whom I have believed and am persuaded that He is able to keep what I have committed to Him until that Day" (2 Tim. 1:12, NKJV). Believing in God is a fundamental prerequisite to knowing Him.

The Bible says, "Faith is the substance of things hoped for, the evidence of things not seen" (Heb. 11:1). Faith gives substance to hope, and it provides us with evidence regarding things that we cannot see, hear, touch, taste, or smell. Jesus said, "Blessed are they that have not seen, and yet have believed" (John 20:29).

The heart of faith knows God. The hand of faith clings to Him. The arms of faith embrace Him.

Faith Knows No Limits

Biblical faith knows God as the One who is: ". . able to do exceedingly abundantly above all that we ask or think, according to the power that works in us" (Eph. 3:20, NKJV). Faith knows no limits because it perceives God as the One who can do all things. It agrees with Jesus who said, ". . .with God all things are possible" (Matt. 19:26, NKJV).

Faith is positive, certain, sure. It takes action toward God, through God, and with God. It is the response of our total self – spirit, will, intellect, emotions – to our heavenly Father. Faith results in a renewed outlook, attitude, and confidence in the believer's life.

Faith incorporates what we believe into what we live. It lets God's power move in our behalf, and it makes His presence in our lives real. Oswald Chambers puts it this way: "This life of faith is not a life of mounting up with

wings, but a life of walking and not fainting."
Faith is definitely a matter of our walking as
well as our talking. James said, ". . .faith by
itself, if it does not have works, is dead"
(James 2:17, NKJV). Faith will inevitably
result in corresponding action.

Faith is believing what God says. It
doesn't simply involve believing that God can
do something; it is actually believing that He
will do it, or that He has already
accomplished it.

As we learn to trust God for the
seemingly impossible, we get to know more
of God in all of His power and glory.

Speaking Our Faith

In the preceding chapter we learned that
faith comes to us through the Word of God.
As we let His Word have its place in our lives,
we learn to speak its truth to our hearts and
to others. This accomplishes great and mighty
things as we grow in our knowledge of God.

Paul wrote, "The word is near you, in
your mouth and in your heart (that is, the
word of faith which we preach): that if you
confess with your mouth the Lord Jesus and
believe in your heart that God has raised Him
from the dead, you will be saved. For with
the heart one believes unto righteousness,
and with the mouth confession is made unto

salvation. For the Scripture says, 'Whoever believes on Him will not be put to shame.'" (Rom. 10:8-11, NKJV).

As we remember that the Word is the Father speaking to us, we are emboldened to speak the Word with conviction and power. This is faith in action, because it is the word of faith proceeding directly from the heart of our Father through us. Jesus always acted on His Father's words, and we must do the same.

Faith knows the truth of these words: "Thou shalt find him [God], if thou seek him with all thy heart and with all thy soul" (Deut. 4:29).

Dr. Bill Bright, founder of Campus Crusade for Christ, provides us with a thought-provoking illustration of how faith is an integral part of knowing God: "My wife and I have two grown sons. Suppose that when they were little boys they had come to greet me when I returned home from a trip and said, 'We love you. We missed you. We are so excited about your being home. We have been talking together and we have decided that we will do anything you want us to do. From now on, you issue the command and we will obey without any questions. We just want to please you.'

"What do you think would have been my attitude in response to their expressions of love for me? If I had responded the way many people think God will respond if they said to Him, 'Lord, I'll do anything you want me to do. I'll go anywhere you want me to go,' I would have taken them by the shoulders, looked at them with an evil eye and said, 'I have just been waiting for you to say that. Now I'm going to make you regret your decision to trust as long as you live. I am going to take all the fun out of your lives. I will make you miserable as long as you live.'

"No, I wouldn't have said that. I would have put my arms around them and given them a big hug and said, 'Zac, Brad, I love you, too, and want to justify your faith in me. I want to be a better father to you. I want to do everything I can to help you find full and meaningful lives.'"

God loves us with an everlasting love. He wants the best for us. Knowing God through faith, then, is knowing Him as our loving Father, full of grace, who has unlimited power and is willing to move in our behalf. This is the only kind of faith that the Bible recognizes.

Knowing God Through Obedience

Jesus said, "Thou shalt love the Lord thy God with all thy heart, and with all thy soul, and with all thy mind. This is the first and great commandment" (Matt. 22:37-38). The reason why Jesus was able to say that this is the supreme commandment is because He knows that when we have this one in place in our lives, there won't be a problem with keeping the other commandments.

In this commandment Jesus is telling us that we must love our Father in heaven with every aspect of our being. Such an all-encompassing love can only come through a deep, personal relationship with our Father which makes keeping all the commandments a joy. St. Augustine said, "Love God, and do what thou wilt." Encapsulated in this short statement is the profound understanding that one who truly loves God will always choose to obey Him.

Jesus said this as well: "He who has My commandments and keeps them, it is he who loves Me. And he who loves Me will be loved by My Father, and I will love him and manifest Myself to him" (John 14:21, NKJV). One mark of our love for Jesus and the Father is our obedience to God's commandments. As we obey the Father, Jesus will manifest himself to us. As He does this our fellowship with Him will grow. Our obedience is a pathway to intimacy with God.

The commandments of God stem from His great love for us, and they teach us a great deal about the character of our Father. Most earthly fathers strive for the best for their children, and that's why they have certain expectations of their children. Those expectations (or commandments) are not for the good of the father; they're for the good of the children. The same is true with the commandments of God.

God says, "Do them [the commandments], that ye may live" (Deut. 4:1). Our obedience to God's commands imparts life to us. They also give us wisdom: "Keep therefore and do them; for this is your wisdom and your understanding in the sight of the nations" (Deut. 4:6).

God does not impose the commandments upon us in order to make our lives miserable. He gives them to us to make our lives happier and more worthwhile. He knows that the commandments will keep us safe, if we will heed them and do them.

Obedience Brings Blessing to Us

The Bible says, "Do them [the commandments], that ye may prosper in all that ye do" (Deut. 29:9). God wants to bless us and prosper us, as John puts forth in his letter: "Beloved, I pray that you may prosper in all things and be in health, just as your soul prospers" (3 John 2, NKJV).

This truth is developed for us by Joshua: "This Book of the Law shall not depart from your mouth, but you shall meditate in it day and night, that you may observe to do according to all that is written in it. For then you will make your way prosperous, and then you will have good success" (Josh. 1:8, NKJV). God promises us prosperity and success when we obey His commandments.

George Eliot puts it this way: "How will you find good? It is not a thing of choices; it is a river that flows from the foot of the invisible throne, and flows by the path of obedience." Obedience is a river of life, success, prosperity, and blessedness from God's heart to ours. This is what our Father wants for us, and this is why we must learn to obey Him in all things.

Isaiah wrote, "If ye be willing and obedient, ye shall eat the good of the land" (Isa. 1:19). God wants us to enjoy the good things of life, and He wants us to have peace and prosperity. It has been well said that, "It is not *after* keeping God's commandments, but *in* keeping them that there is great reward." God has linked these two things together, and no one can separate them.

God's commandments are perfect; they convert the soul. God's commandments are sure; they give wisdom to the simple-minded. God's commandments are right; they cause our hearts to rejoice. God's commandments are pure; they enlighten our eyes. God's commandments are true and righteous; they are to be desired more than the finest gold. God's commandments are sweet; they warn us. Obeying God's commandments is wonderful, because it brings us great reward. (See Ps. 19:7-11.)

Obedience Pleases the Father

As we obey the Father, we increase in our knowledge of Him. Paul wrote, "That ye might walk worthy of the Lord unto all pleasing, being fruitful in every good work, and increasing in the knowledge of God" (Col. 1:10). To increase in the knowledge of God, therefore, we must obey Him. This pleases our Father very much.

God answers the prayers of His obedient children, as John tells us: "And whatsoever we ask, we receive of him, because we keep his commandments, and do those things that are pleasing in his sight" (1 John 3:22). This is what God wants for each of us – to learn that He is pleased by our obedience, and that He will answer our prayers when we walk in obedience.

To obey God is perfect liberty. As we obey, we shall experience freedom, safety, and happiness. Happiness, for the believer, comes through obedience. Peace, for the believer, comes through obedience. Freedom, for the believer, comes through obedience. Prosperity, for the believer, comes through obedience. Success, for the believer, comes through obedience.

Knowing the Father comes, in large measure, through obedience. Pleasing the Father is accomplished, in large measure, through willing obedience.

> *And whatsoever we ask, we receive*
> *of him, because we keep his*
> *commandments, and do those things*
> *that are pleasing in his sight.*
> (1 John 3:22)

Prayer Response: Dear God, my loving Father, I know that you are able to do all things, and that you do all things well. I express faith to you now that you will move in my behalf in the following areas:_____

_____.

Because I know you intimately through faith I desire with all my heart to obey you fully. Continue your workmanship in my life, Father, so that I will always be your obedient child. In Jesus' name I pray, Amen.

11

KNOWING GOD THROUGH PRAYER

*Be careful for nothing; but in every
thing by prayer and supplication with
thanksgiving let your requests be
made known unto God. And the
peace of God, which passeth all
understanding, shall keep your
hearts and minds through Christ Jesus.*
(Phil. 4:6-7)

Prayer Is Fellowship With God

Prayer is the primary way in which we initiate fellowship with our heavenly Father. There are many different kinds of prayer and many different modes of prayer, such as asking prayer, seeking prayer, devotional prayer, the prayer of agreement, the prayer of faith, intercessory prayer, spiritual-warfare prayer, praying in the Spirit, prayer of consecration, etc. We won't be analyzing each of these in this chapter, but we will emphasize several keys to knowing God intimately through prayer. This will show you how to have fellowship with your heavenly Father.

The first of these keys is faith. When the Bible says, "Be anxious for nothing, but in everything by prayer and supplication with thanksgiving, let your requests be made known unto God," it is showing us the avenue to vital fellowship with God through prayer. Anxiety over anything separates us from fellowship with God, because it is not based on faith, and ". . .without faith, it is impossible to please him" (Heb. 11:6). Anxiety is a form of fear, and it indicates that our focus is on our troubles instead of God's help.

God wants you to give Him all your anxieties, "casting all your care upon Him, for He cares for you" (1 Pet. 5:7, NKJV). Giving our anxieties and cares to Him is an act of faith and trust. Giving Him our anxieties, telling Him our needs, and thanking Him express our faith and trust. This quiets our noisy soul and opens the door to His peace.

Thanksgiving is the second key to fellowshipping with God. Thankfulness is a wellspring of joy. It "cuts off at the pass" all fear, anger, resentment, bitterness, loneliness, depression, and despair. Remember, "A merry heart doeth good like a medicine: but a broken spirit drieth the bones" (Prov. 17:22). Even medical practitioners who are not Christian believers have long recognized the healing power of joy and mirth. It is actually one of the best medicines available today.

Friendship is a third key to knowing God intimately through prayer. Friends know each other well enough to realize what each other enjoys, believes, desires, dreams, and hopes. One friend knows the other's aspirations and even his or her thoughts. True friends never take each other for granted; they always endeavor to nurture and cherish the relationship. It is the same when we are fellowshipping with God through prayer. We don't just go to Him with our needs and desires, or even our concerns for others and the world we live in. We come to share the things He cares about, as well as the things we care about.

Fellowship with God through prayer deepens when we realize He calls us His friends. (See John 15:14-15.) As we come to Him on a friend-to-Friend basis, we ask Him what He thinks, and what His plans and purposes are. It is here that we listen for His response. As we enter into this kind of fellowship with the Father we find that our desire is not merely to ask Him for things but to know Him and love Him.

It is in the nature of friendship that each friend will draw something precious from the other, and sometimes close friends may even exchange extravagant gifts. They love each other for the fellowship they enjoy together. They give to each other because they love each other. We get to know God in this kind of intimate way through His Word, prayer, and by His Spirit.

This leads us to another key to prayer. It is the Word of God. It is by studying His Word that you will get to know the heart of God. When your fellowship in prayer with Him is based upon the Word, you will be sure to say the things with which you know He will agree. It is as if God is saying to us, *"If you will come to Me in faith, with a grateful heart, knowing My heart and saying the things I say about you and your circumstances through My Word, there is no limit to where our mutual friendship will take you, and what I will be able to do for you."*

As God answers your prayers, you will experience His peace, and this will draw you ever closer to your heavenly Friend.

With this background in view, let's take a good look at the many things God's Word has to say about prayer and fellowship. This chapter will enrich your understanding, and you will begin to see for yourself things about prayer and fellowship with God that you may have missed before.

A Letter From the Father to You

I promise to be near to you when you call unto Me.[1] Your prayer is My delight.[2] As you seek Me, you will find Me, when you seek Me with all your heart.[3] Call unto Me, and I will answer you, and show you great and mighty things that you do not know.[4]

Always remember that I know the things you need even before you express them to Me.[5] As you ask, it shall be given to you. When you seek, you will find. When you knock, the door will be opened unto you.[6] When you ask, you shall receive.[7] When you pray in the name of Jesus, I promise I will answer you.[8]

As you ask, you shall receive so that your joy will be full.[9] Pray without ceasing.[10] Remember that your effectual, fervent prayer will always avail much.[11]

I know your heart, beloved.[12] All of your works are known to Me.[13] I search your heart.[14] Indeed, I know all things.[15]

You are My precious child.[16] I take great pleasure in you.[17] I have chosen you.[18] Because you have received Jesus as your Savior, I have adopted you into My family.[19] You are My greatly loved child as a result of your faith in Christ Jesus.[20]

Remember, My child, that I will keep you as the apple of My eye, and I will hide you under the shadow of My wings.[21] My child, I promise never to fail you nor forsake you.[22]

References: (1) Psalms 145:18; (2) Proverbs 15:8; (3) Jeremiah 29:13; (4) Jeremiah 33:3; (5) Matthew 6:8; (6) Matthew 7:7; (7) Matthew 7:8; (8) John 16:23; (9) John 16:24; (10) 1 Thessalonians 5:17; (11) James 5:16; (12) 1 Chronicles 28:9; (13) Psalms 1:6; (14) Luke 16:15; (15) 1 John 3:20; (16) Deuteronomy 14:1; (17) Psalms 149:4; (18) Isaiah 41:9; (19) John 1:12; (20) Galatians 3:26; (21) Psalms 17:8; (22) Deuteronomy 31:6.

Conversing With God

Every relationship in our lives requires good communication, and this is certainly true of our relationship with God. Prayer is our line of communication with our heavenly Father. Jeremiah wrote, "Call to Me, and I will answer you, and show you great and mighty things, which you do not know" (Jer. 33:3, NKJV).

We call to God. He answers us, and He shows us what we need to know. This dynamic process includes both active listening and speaking, and it may even include silence as we wait before the Father.

God is only a prayer away, and to know Him we must go to Him in prayer. Prayer is a conversation with God in which He tells us His concerns, lays out His plans and purposes for us, reveals truth to us, and expresses His love to us. It is a remarkable conversation in that it helps us to understand our Father and His ways as we share our love, concerns, and hopes with Him.

Andrew Murray defines prayer as: ". . .not monologue, but dialogue; God's voice in response to mine is its most essential part. Listening to God's voice is the secret of the assurance that He will listen to mine."

How do we hear what God is saying? Most often it is an impression, a knowing, or a small voice within our hearts. For the Prophet Elijah, it was a "still small voice" (1 Kings 19:12). Jesus said, "My sheep hear My voice, and I know them, and they follow Me" (John 10:27, NKJV). This is a great truth. God has placed within our hearts the ability to actually hear His voice.

One Sunday afternoon several years ago we were home alone, when Kathleen sensed God speaking to her heart. She said, "I think God just told me that Bill and Mary don't have any food, and that we are supposed to go to their house and help them." Wanting to be obedient, and hoping that it really was the

Lord who had spoken, we drove to Bill and Mary's home.

Kathleen and Mary went into the kitchen to talk. After a few moments, Kathleen asked her, "Well, what did you have for lunch today?" Somewhat embarrassed, Mary responded, "We are out of money, and the only food we had in the house was two pieces of bread and three carrots. I sautéed the carrots and served them with the bread to Bill and the children."

Aware of their need and God's voice of direction, we were grateful to have this opportunity to be of help. Bill and Mary expressed their great appreciation for the food we then bought for them, and we all thanked God for His love and faithfulness.

Prayer Promises

The power of prayer is backed with the full faithfulness and authority of our heavenly Father. His Word is filled with promises about prayer. Through these promises we get to understand God so much better. As we claim these special promises for our own lives, we enter an entirely new dimension of living. We obtain these promises through believing prayer. Some of God's prayer promises to us are cited below:

"I will call on the Lord, who is worthy to be praised: so shall I be saved from mine enemies" (2 Sam. 22:4). Through prayer we learn that God is our Defender.

"In my distress I called upon the Lord, and cried to my God: and he did hear my voice out of his temple, and my cry did enter into his ears" (2 Sam. 22:7). When we pray we know that God will hear our prayers.

"Thus saith the Lord, the God of David thy father, I have heard thy prayer, I have seen thy tears: behold, I will heal thee" (2 Kings 20:5). Through prayer we discover that God knows our deepest feelings and all our wounds, and He is our Healer.

"I sought the Lord, and he heard me, and delivered me from all my fears" (Ps. 34:4). Prayer helps us to know that God will take our fears from us.

"This poor man cried, and the Lord heard him, and saved him out of all his troubles" (Ps. 34:6). In response to our prayers God intervenes to help us solve our problems.

"Offer unto God thanksgiving; and pay thy vows unto the most High: And call upon me in the day of trouble: I will deliver thee, and thou shalt glorify me" (Ps. 50:14-15). Through prayer we discover God as our Deliverer.

"He shall call upon me, and I will answer him: I will be with him in trouble; I will deliver him, and honour him. With long life will I satisfy him, and shew him my salvation" (Ps. 91:15-16). God promises to answer our prayers, to be with us, to honor us, and to give us a long life.

"The Lord is nigh unto all them that call upon him, to all that call upon him in truth" (Ps. 145:18). As we pray, God promises to be near us.

"Your Father knoweth what things ye have need of, before ye ask him" (Matt. 6:8). God knows all of our needs, even before we express them to Him, but He wants us to express them to Him nonetheless. Why? Because He responds to faith, not to need alone. Faith is a spiritual action; need is merely a natural condition. Faith is the currency of God's kingdom. It's God's way, and it is the best possible way.

"And all things, whatsoever ye shall ask in prayer, believing, ye shall receive" (Matt. 21:22). Here, Jesus himself explains that faith is a key component of prayer. It enables us to receive what we ask for, because we believe God will answer. God responds to faith expressed through prayer.

"Hitherto have ye asked nothing in my name: ask, and ye shall receive, that your joy may be full" (John 16:24). When we pray in Jesus' name, God will answer our prayer and we will be joyful.

"Let us therefore come boldly unto the throne of grace, that we may obtain mercy, and find grace to help in time of need" (Heb. 4:16). Without hesitation, we can be sure that we will receive mercy and grace from the Father's hand.

"For the eyes of the Lord are over the righteous, and his ears are open unto their prayers" (1 Pet. 3:12). God sees us, and He is listening for our prayers.

"And this is the confidence that we have in him, that, if we ask any thing according to his will, he heareth us. And if we know that he hear us, whatsoever we ask, we know that we have the petitions that we desired of him" (1 John 5:14-15). God hears us when we pray according to His will, and when we know this, we can be sure that He will grant our petitions.

Notice how each of these promises, and a multitude of other ones as well, reiterate time and time again the fact that *God hears us*. Unless we believe this, there is no need to pray, but when we do believe that He hears us, we enter into exciting, new spiritual perspectives.

It is advisable to write down each of the requests we bring before the Father, and then, next to each one, to record His answers. This helps us to see how God is always intervening in our lives, and how He loves to hear and answer our prayers. Knowing God as our prayer-answering Father is one of the greatest joys of life.

"For all the promises of God in him are yea, and in him Amen, unto the glory of God by us" (2 Cor. 1:20).

Incorporating the promises into our prayer life, by praying the Word of God, brings us into an intimacy with God that is impossible any other way. Peter writes, "Grace and peace be multiplied to you in the knowledge of God and of Jesus our Lord, as His divine power has given to us all things that pertain to life and godliness, through the knowledge of Him who called us by glory and virtue, by which have been given to us exceedingly great and precious promises, that through these you may be partakers of the divine nature, having escaped the corruption that is in the world through lust" (2 Pet. 1:2-4, NKJV).

Peter so wanted the believers to know God. His prayer was that grace and peace would be multiplied to us as we get to know God more fully. He explains that Almighty God has given us all things pertaining to life and godliness as a result of knowing Him. He goes on to show how it is God's promises that enable us to partake of the very nature of God himself.

Peter then delineates some attributes of the divine nature: diligence, faith, virtue, knowledge, self-control, perseverance, godliness, brotherly kindness, and love. These qualities sound remarkably close to the fruit of the Holy Spirit in our lives, as outlined by Paul in his letter to the Galatians: "But the fruit of the Spirit is love, joy, peace, longsuffering, kindness, goodness, faithfulness, gentleness, self-control" (Gal. 5:22-23, NKJV).

This list of spiritual fruit that are supplied by the Holy Spirit, gives us a fairly clear picture of God's nature. He is love, joy, and peace. He is patient and kind. He is filled with goodness, faithfulness, gentleness, and self-control. Through prayer, focused on the promises of His Word and empowered by the Holy Spirit, we can partake of that same wonderful nature. It is impossible to do so otherwise.

Visiting With Our Father

God calls us to prayer. He invites us to visit with Him. Prayer opens the door into His chambers where we can sit with Him and learn about Him.

Imagine if the world's leading expert in a particular field of study or other endeavor that we find important were to invite us into his or her study for conversation. How excited we would be at that prospect! How many questions would we ask this person we hold in such high esteem? Would we do most of the talking, or would we become avid listeners?

Such an invitation has been extended to us by our heavenly Father — the Creator of the universe — who wants to spend time with us. He welcomes us with open arms.

This is an open invitation. We do not have to make an appointment to see our heavenly Father, because He operates with an open-door policy. He says, *"Come in and spend time with Me. I want you to be with Me. I have many things to share with you."*

R.A. Torrey wrote, "Our whole life should be a life of prayer. We should walk in constant communion with God. There should be a constant looking upward to God. We should walk so habitually in His presence that even when we awake in the night it would be the most natural thing for us to speak to Him in thanksgiving or petition."

How to Pray

The Bible says, "The effective, fervent prayer of a righteous man avails much" (James 5:16, NKJV). Fervency in prayer is a vitally important matter. It means that our prayers will be heart-felt, warm, and impassioned, and they will exhibit deep and sincere emotions. A fervent prayer is a faith-filled, believing prayer.

For our prayers to be effectual, therefore, they must be fervent, but an effectual prayer is also one that is effective, brings results, and bears fruit. Effectual prayers pave the way for God's answers.

A medical missionary in Africa learned about the power of believing prayer through a little girl in her orphanage. The doctor had spent an entire night working hard to help a mother in the labor ward, but in spite of all efforts, the woman died, leaving behind a premature infant and a crying two-year-old daughter.

The missionary realized it would be difficult to keep the baby alive since they did not have an incubator. In fact, there was no electricity to run an incubator. The real need was for a hot water bottle to keep the baby warm. Even though the mission compound was on the Equator, the nights could get quite chilly.

They wrapped the baby in the warmest materials available, while the doctor searched for a hot water bottle. When the bottle was found, a nurse attendant was asked to fill it. She came running back to the missionary in a few moments, however, to let her know that the water bottle had burst as she was filling it! "And it is our last hot water bottle!" she exclaimed.

The following morning the missionary went to have prayers with the children in the orphanage. She gave the children various prayer requests, including the need for a hot water bottle for the newborn. She also mentioned the two-year-old sister who was crying for her mother.

A ten-year-old girl named Ruth heard the prayer requests, and she led out in prayer: "Please, God, send us a water bottle. It'll be no good tomorrow, God, as the baby will be dead, so please send it this afternoon."

The missionary gasped inwardly at the audacity of Ruth's prayer. Then the girl continued, "And while You are about it, would You please send a dolly for the little girl so she'll know you really love her?"

The missionary was not sure if she could even say Amen to this heart-felt prayer, but she did so, even though she wasn't at all certain that the prayer would be answered. After all, she had been there for four years and had never received a package of any kind. She said to herself, "Oh, yes, I know that God can do every thing. The Bible says He can, but there are limits!"

Even if a package were to arrive that afternoon, it was highly unlikely that someone would send a hot water bottle to equatorial Africa! That afternoon, as the missionary was teaching in the nurses' training school, a message was sent that a car had come to the entrance of the compound. On the verandah of her house she found a twenty-two-pound parcel! Tears began to well up in her eyes as she sent for the orphanage children.

They rushed to her house, as she struggled to open the package. As they unwrapped the paper, and pulled off the string, excitement began to mount. First, the missionary lifted out some colorful jerseys, and the eyes of the children sparkled as she distributed the shirts to them. Then she took out knitted bandages for the leprosy patients, and the children began to get bored.

She shared some snacks that she found in the box with the children, and then she put her hand back into the parcel. Could it really be? The next item was a brand-new, rubber hot water bottle. The missionary cried.

Ruth, standing in the front of forty children, did not seem at all surprised. She rushed forward and shouted, "If God has sent the bottle, He must have sent the dolly too." She proceeded to rummage through the box. On the bottom she found the second answer to her prayer – a small, beautifully dressed dolly. She turned to the missionary and asked, "Can I go over with you, and give this dolly to that little girl so she'll really know Jesus loves her?" The missionary quickly agreed, and off they went, with great joy and thankfulness in their hearts.

The parcel had been shipped five months before! It had been packed by the missionary's former Sunday school class whose leader had heard and obeyed God, prompting her to send a hot water bottle to the Equator. And one of the girls had put a dolly in the box for an unknown African child. This all happened five months before the believing prayer of a ten-year-old girl who had asked that the needs would be met "that afternoon."

Isaiah wrote these words of God: "Before they call, I will answer" (Isa. 65:24). This wonderful testimony reveals the truth of that statement, and shows how God works to meet our needs in answer to our prayers.

Effectual praying, according to the Bible, is:

Praying in Faith. "Therefore I say unto you, What things soever ye desire, when ye pray, *believe* that ye receive them, and ye shall have them" (Mark 11:24).

Praying God's Word. "And this is the confidence that we have in him, that, if we ask any thing according to his will [as it is revealed in His Word], he heareth us: And if we know that he hear us, whatsoever we ask, we know that we have the petitions that we desired of him" (1 John 5:14-15).

Praying in the Name of Jesus. Jesus said, "If ye shall ask any thing in my name, I will do it" (John 14:14).

Praying with Persistence. "Pray without ceasing" (1 Thess. 5:17).

Praying for Specific Things. "Whosoever . . .shall not doubt in his heart, but shall believe that *those things* which he saith shall come to pass; he shall have whatsoever he saith" (Mark 11:23).

Praying in Humility. "If my people, which are called by my name, shall humble themselves, and pray, and seek my face, and turn from their wicked ways; then will I hear from heaven, and will forgive their sin, and will heal their land" (2 Chron. 7:14).

Praying in the Spirit. "With all prayer and supplication in the Spirit, and watching thereunto with all perseverance and supplication for all the saints" (Eph. 6:18).

Waiting on God. "Thou shalt know that I am the Lord: for they shall not be ashamed that wait for me" (Isa. 49:23).

Thanksgiving and Praise. "Enter into his gates with thanksgiving, and into his courts with praise: be thankful unto him, and bless his name" (Ps. 100:4).

Abiding in Christ. Jesus said, "If ye abide in me, and my words abide in you, ye shall ask what ye will, and it shall be done unto you" (John 15:7).

Absolute Surrender. Jesus prayed, "Father, if you are willing, take this cup from me; yet not my will, but yours, be done" (Luke 22:42, NIV).

Priorities. "But seek first the kingdom of God and His righteousness, and all these things shall be added unto you" (Matt. 6:33, NKJV).

Trusting in God. "Trust in the Lord with all thine heart; and lean not unto thine own understanding. In all thy ways acknowledge him, and he shall direct thy paths" (Prov. 3:5-6).

Praying With a Forgiving Heart. Jesus said, "Therefore, if you are offering your gift at the altar and there remember that your brother has something against you, leave your gift there in front of the altar. First go and be reconciled to your brother; then come and offer your gift" (Matt. 5:23-24, NIV).

Praying in Agreement. Jesus said, "If two of you agree on earth concerning anything that they ask, it will be done for them by my Father in heaven. For where two or three are gathered together in My name, I am there in the midst of them" (Matt. 18:19-20, NKJV).

Praying in Obedience. "And whatsoever we ask, we receive of him, because we keep his commandments, and do those things that are pleasing in his sight" (1 John 3:22).

Active Listening. "Your ears shall hear a word behind you, saying, 'This is the way, walk in it'" (Isa. 30:21, NKJV).

The preceding list covers only a few of the important aspects of effectual praying, many of which relate to the attitudes of our heart. Other attitudes that enhance our prayer life include love, joy, peace, hope, compassion, trust, and confidence.

Charles G. Finney defines effectual prayer as follows: "Prevailing, or effectual prayer, is that prayer which attains the blessing that it seeks. It is that prayer which effectively moves God. The very idea of effectual prayer is that it affects its object."

E.M. Bounds explains it this way: "True prayer that wins an answer must be backed up by a scriptural, vital, personal religion. They are the essentials of real Christian service in this life. Of these requirements the most important is that in serving, we serve. So in praying, we must talk with God. Truth and heart reality, these are the core, the substance, the sum, the heart of prayer. Prayer has no potential unless we pray with simplicity, sincerity, and truth."

Prayer puts us in touch with God. It is a strong link in the chain that binds our hearts to Him, and enables us to know Him as He truly is. To know Him intimately we must pray and pray and pray.

Maintaining Our Fellowship
With the Father

Oswald Chambers writes, "We do not know what God's compelling purpose is, but whatever happens, we must maintain our relationship with Him. We must never allow anything to damage our relationship with God, but if something does damage it, we must take the time to make it right again. The most important aspect of Christianity is not the work we do, but the relationship we maintain and the surrounding influence and qualities produced by that relationship. That is all God asks us to give our attention to, and it is the one thing that is continually under attack."

In the Introduction of the book, we cited the statement from the Westminster Catechism: "The chief end of man is to glorify God, and to enjoy Him forever." To enjoy God we must know Him.

It is often said that we become like the person we spend the most time with. In fact, we do pick up their mannerisms and values as a part of our relationship with them. The same is true in our relationship with God.

The more we spend time with Him, the more we become like Him.

That hits home, doesn't it? Perhaps He is leading us to lay aside less important things that take up our time so that we could and would spend that time with Him. Spend time with Him, adore Him, pray to Him, get alone with Him, express your love to Him, glorify Him, and let Him be God, the Father, to you. He will love you, sustain you, bless you, heal you, lead you, protect you, guide you, help you, encourage you, provide for you, restore you, and take care of you as His child forever.

The blossoming of love in a young couple is a beautiful thing to behold. The budding relationship imparts great hope, excitement, and anticipation in the hearts of the two who love each other. Just the thought of being able to spend time with the one we love brings great joy to us.

Our relationship with God should be exactly like this. As His beloved, we should eagerly anticipate every single moment that we are able to spend with Him. He is our Beloved, and we are His beloved.

The Song of Solomon creates a vivid verbal picture of our all-encompassing relationship with our God by comparing it to the relationship experienced by two people in love. We want God to draw us to Him, and like the daughters of Jerusalem, we shout, "We will run after you!" (Song of Sol. 1:4, NKJV).

As our Beloved draws us closer to Him, we are impelled to run toward Him. James writes, "Draw near to God and He will draw near to you" (James 4:8, NKJV). As the King invites us into His chambers for the purpose of intimate, loving fellowship, we "will be glad and rejoice" in Him (Song of Sol. 1:4, NKJV).

We are in His presence, and we are hearing His voice. This is fellowship, and this is the most blessed communion that life has to offer. "He brought me to the banqueting house, and his banner over me was love" (Song of Sol. 2:4, NKJV).

This is what fellowship with the Father is like, and it causes us to sing with certainty, "I am my beloved's, and my beloved is mine" (Song of Sol. 6:3, NKJV).

We are speaking here of the wonderful love that God has for us and we can have for Him. These are the deep wonders of His love where we encounter God heart to heart. This is where deep calls unto deep (See Ps. 42:7), and the interactions transcend the natural sphere of life. This is His desire and His will for us; a spiritual reality that is only available to those who belong to His kingdom and His family. The world will never see it.

Prayer Response: Heavenly Father, I love you, and I enjoy spending time in prayer and fellowship with you. In such times of sweet intimacy I feel renewed, loved, cared for, and strengthened. Thank you for giving me this means of getting to know you better. Through your grace, Father, I will pray without ceasing, rejoice evermore, and give thanks in everything. Thank you for hearing me and answering my prayers. In Jesus' name, Amen.

Publisher's Note: To learn more about the core dimensions of effective praying, you are encouraged to read the following titles published by Victory House, Inc.: *Prayers That Prevail, Prayers That Prevail for Your Children, More Prayers That Prevail, Mini Prayers That Prevail, Praying Bible Promises, Bible Prayers for All Your Needs, Believers' Prayers and Promises, Breakthrough Prayers for Women* and *Prayer Keys*.

12

KNOWING GOD THROUGH PRAISE AND WORSHIP

*All the earth shall worship You and
sing praises to You; they shall sing
praises to Your name. Come and see
the works of God; He is awesome in
His doing toward the sons of men.*
(Ps. 66:4-5, NKJV)

Praising God With Exuberant Joy

Often, the words "praise" and "worship" are used interchangeably. Many dictionaries even denote these two terms as being synonymous. However, the Scriptures make a clear distinction between these two avenues to knowing God.

Praise is associated with exuberant joy and thanksgiving. It is our response to all that God has done for us. Worship, on the other hand, is the expression of reverential awe in the presence of God's glory and holiness. It is our response to the recognition of who God is.

As we praise God for what He has done for us, our eyes are opened to see Him as being more than our Father and our Provider.

Praise, as we enter His presence, helps us to see God as our King and Creator, the awesome and holy sovereign Lord.

Praise is an attitude of our hearts. It is not just an action we engage in during church services or private devotions. It is a state of being – an actual life-style. David said, "His praise shall *continually* be in my mouth" (Ps. 34:1). The writer of the Hebrews develops this thought as well: "By Him [Jesus] let us *continually* offer the sacrifice of praise to God, that is the fruit of our lips, giving thanks to His name" (Heb. 13:15, NKJV).

How and when to praise our King? Audibly, and at all times. To praise Him should be as natural as breathing is.

As we have already seen, the name of Jesus represents all that God is to us. His name is our key to redemption, and our access to all of His promises. The name of Jesus should command our constant attention, issuing in continual praise. Without His name, we would be lost, hopeless, and wretched beyond measure, but when our minds are fixed on all that Jesus' name represents, our hearts rise with praise and thanksgiving to the Lord.

There are many ways to praise God, but they all involve both thanksgiving and joy.

David even danced before the Lord with all his might as an act of praise. (See 2 Sam. 6:14.) We may clap our hands, and shout. (See Ps. 47:1.) We make a joyful noise unto the Lord as we serve Him with gladness, and come before His presence with singing. (See Ps. 100.) We may even lift up our hands unto Him. (See Ps. 63:4.) Regardless of which praise posture or behavior we employ, our purpose in praise is to acknowledge and honor the goodness of our God. People sometimes have difficulty about any exuberant expression to God. They might be able to get excited about other things in life, but not God. This is usually because their conditioning in earlier years has taught them to be always sober and quiet when they go before God.

Abandonment and surrender to God are where true praise begins. Continual praise comes from a heart that is aware of God's presence everywhere. We can practice His presence through praise wherever we go – in the car, while washing the dishes, as we mow the grass, while walking or jogging, or even in conversation. Praise is not something that is only reserved for church services or daily devotions.

Worship, like praise, takes the focus off ourselves and puts it on God. David wrote,

"O worship the Lord in the beauty of holiness: fear before him, all the earth" (Ps. 96:9). This is a profound statement, and it entails many things.

Worship recognizes the awesome beauty of God's holiness, but it also recognizes that true worship flows from the beauty of holiness within the worshiper. Our holiness is a product of the indwelling Holy Spirit, and God finds our holiness to be absolutely beautiful, just as we find His holiness to be absolutely beautiful.

Richard J. Foster, in his excellent book, *Celebration of Discipline*, writes, "God is actively seeking worshipers. . . .Worship is our response to the overtures of love from the heart of the Father, . . .but we have not worshiped the Lord until Spirit touches spirit. . . .Our spirit must be ignited by the divine fire."

Jesus said, "God is Spirit, and those who worship Him must worship in spirit and in truth" (John 4:24, NKJV). To know God intimately is to have our spirit touched by the Spirit of the One who is love. Truly, to worship Him is to be lost in His love. In such a place, we can immerse ourselves in praise and worship of God, without reference to anything else happening around us or in us.

Here we become the answer to Jesus' prayer –
one in and with our God.

As you read the following pages, we pray
that your spirit will be touched by the Spirit
of God, and that you will be lifted into new
realms of praise and worship as you see God
revealed in all His wonder, power, and glory.

A Letter From the Father to You:

Praise Me, and sing unto Me, because I
have triumphed gloriously.[1] Ascribe greatness
to Me.[2] Give Me glory.[3] When you do these
things it blesses both Me and you, My child.[4]

Give thanks unto Me.[5] Praise Me, because
My mercy endures forever.[6] Stand up and
bless Me forever.[7]

When you offer praise to Me you glorify
Me.[8] Let your mouth be filled with praise all
day long.[9] It is a good thing to give thanks
unto Me, and to sing praise to Me.[10]

Seek My face.[11] Worship and serve Me
only.[12]

Wait upon Me, beloved. Be of good
courage, and I will strengthen your heart. Wait
upon Me.[13] Walk after Me, my child, and give
reverence to Me. Keep My commandments,
and obey My voice.[14] Love Me, and walk in
all My ways. Keep My commandments and

cleave to Me. Serve Me with all your heart and soul.[15]

If you want to know what it is that I require of you, remember these words: reverence Me and walk in all My ways. Love Me, and serve Me with all your heart and all your soul.[16]

Make a joyful noise to Me. Serve Me with gladness, and come before My presence with singing. Enter into My gates with thanksgiving, and into My courts with praise. Be thankful unto Me, and bless My name.[17] I love it when you worship Me in spirit and in truth.[18] Be still and know that I am your God.[19]

References: (1) Exodus 15:1; (2) Deuteronomy 32:3; (3) Psalms 29:2; (4) Psalms 50:23; (5) Psalms 147:7; (6) Psalms 136:9; (7) Nehemiah 9:5; (8) Psalms 50:23; (9) Psalms 71:8; (10) Psalms 92:1; (11) Psalms 105:4; (12) Matthew 4:10; (13) Psalms 62:5; (14) Joshua 22:5; (15) Deuteronomy 13:4; (16) Deuteronomy 10:12; (17) Psalms 100; (18) John 4:24; (19) Psalms 46:10.

God Is Our King

"Make a joyful shout to the Lord, all you lands! Serve the Lord with gladness; come before His presence with singing. Know that the Lord, He is God; it is He who has made us, and not we ourselves; we are His people and the sheep of His pasture. Enter into His gates with thanksgiving, and into His courts with praise. Be thankful to Him, and bless His name. For the Lord is good; His mercy is everlasting, and His truth endures to all generations" (Ps. 100, NKJV).

Psalm 100 is rich in divine imagery. It shows us how we go into God's gates with thanksgiving, and how we enter His courts with praise. The picture is one of royalty – God, our King, is sitting upon His throne, overseeing His courts. What a beautiful image this is.

Notice, also, that this verse opens with this statement: "Know that the Lord, He is God." There is a clear connection between praise and knowing God.

Certainly we have a great deal for which to be thankful to God. As the Psalmist points out, God is our Lord and Creator and we are His sheep. This is a great cause for thanksgiving and celebration. As we express our thankfulness to God, our Creator and King, He opens His gates for us. He gives us access to His presence.

Then, as thanksgiving turns to praise, we are actually ushered into the King's courts. We become courtiers to our King. A courtier is one who is in attendance when a king's court is assembled. A king's courts are His place of residence as well as a formal assembly of His courtiers.

It is in the king's courts that one finds his counselors, advisors, officers, and family. To gain entrance into God's courts, therefore, is to become a part of a grand reception hosted by our King.

A sovereign's courts are where people go to give him honor and adulation. Within his courts a sovereign gives direction to his people. In the king's courts people gather to find their leader's will, to hear his decisions about important matters related to the kingdom.

The same things happen when we enter God's courts through praise. We get to know Him so much better, because we actually are in His presence and He speaks to us and tells us what we need to know. Through praise we honor Him, and He in turn expresses His love to us, gives us direction, strengthens us, and rewards us.

Praise helps us to know the royal qualities and attributes of our God and King. "God is the King of all the earth: sing ye praises with understanding" (Ps. 47:7).

St. Augustine of Hippo wrote, "Whatever you praise, you praise it because it is good. Only a madman praises what is not good. If you praise an unjust man on account of his injustice, will you not also be unjust? If you praise a thief because he is a thief, will not you also be his accomplice? On the other hand, if you praise a just man on account of his justice, will not you also have a share in his justice through praising him? So then, whatever else we praise, we praise because it is good. And you can have no greater, better, or surer reason for praising God than that He is good. Therefore, praise the Lord, for He is good."

The Psalmist writes, "But thou art holy, O thou that inhabitest the praises of Israel" (Ps. 22:3).

Through praise we learn that God is more than worthy of receiving our praise; He actually is our praise [reason for praise]. "You shall fear the Lord your God; you shall serve Him, and to Him you shall hold fast, and take oaths in His name. He is your praise, and He is your God, who has done for you these great and awesome things which your eyes have seen" (Deut. 10:20-21, NKJV).

God has done great and awesome things for us, and this leads us into praise which in turn leads us into His presence. Because we know that praise opens the doors to God's courts, we can be sure that God is with us when we are praising Him. The manifest presence of God comes to His people through praise, as it did in the worship service described below:

"It came even to pass, as the trumpeters and singers were as one, to make one sound to be heard in praising and thanking the Lord; and when they lifted up their voice with the trumpets and cymbals and instruments of music, and praised the Lord, saying, For he is good; for his mercy endureth for ever: that then the house was filled with a cloud, even the house of the Lord; So that the priests could not stand to minister by reason of the cloud: for the glory of the Lord had filled the house of God" (2 Chron. 5:13-14).

God's glory and presence are revealed to us through praise. Through praise, David discovered the greatness and majesty of God: "Bless the Lord, O my soul. O Lord my God, thou art very great; thou art clothed with honour and majesty" (Ps. 104:1).

Praise Reminds Us of Who God Is and All He Has Done

The Book of Psalms shows us how God reveals himself to us through praise, releases His power to us through praise, and blesses us through praise. The following verses give us insights into the dynamic of praise, and how it works in us and through us to bring us closer to God:

"I will praise thee, O Lord, with my whole heart; I will shew forth all thy marvellous works. I will be glad and rejoice in thee: I will sing praise to thy name, O thou most High" (Ps. 9:1-2). God, most high, takes great delight in our praises, and as we praise Him, great gladness fills our hearts with rejoicing.

"I will sing unto the Lord, because he hath dealt bountifully with me" (Ps. 13:6). The more we reflect on all God has done for us, the more praise becomes a part of our lives.

"I will declare thy name unto my brethren: in the midst of the congregation will I praise thee" (Ps. 22:22). We praise God in front of the heathen as a witness to His greatness, and we praise God in front of fellow-believers, as an encouragement.

Praise not only takes us into the King's courts, but it accomplishes several other purposes as well:

Praise helps us to remember that God is our triumphant and valiant Conqueror: "I will sing unto the Lord, for he hath triumphed gloriously: the horse and his rider hath he thrown into the sea" (Exod. 15:1).

Praise helps us to remember how great our God is. "I will publish the name of the Lord: ascribe ye greatness unto our God" (Deut. 32:3).

Praise exalts our God. "Exalted be the God of the rock of my salvation" (2 Sam. 22:47).

Praise reminds us of God's eternal mercy. "Praise the Lord; for his mercy endureth for ever" (2 Chron. 20:21).

Praise elevates the name of our God. "Blessed be thy glorious name, which is exalted above all blessing and praise" (Neh. 9:5).

Praise magnifies God (makes Him bigger) to us. "I will praise the name of God with a song, and will magnify him with thanksgiving" (Ps. 69:30).

Praise reminds us of the goodness of God. "Oh that men would praise the Lord for his goodness, and for his wonderful works to the children of men!" (Ps. 107:8).

The One Needful Thing

Worship is a main avenue to intimacy with God. It is one of the most important activities for a believer to engage in. Jesus teaches that the Father seeks us to worship Him. (See John 4:23-24.) The love in the heart of God is seeking after you. God wants you to worship Him. God wants you to fellowship with Him. He wants you to come into His presence and enjoy Him. That's what is in the heart of God.

Yes, God seeks us to worship Him. Does this mean simply that He wants us to go to church each week, or is it something more? Clearly, worship is an activity that can take place anywhere, not only in church, because worship involves adoration, respect, reverence, listening, devotion, admiration, and appreciation. True worship, therefore, is conducted in an attitude of humility before the Father. God wants us to worship Him; in fact, He seeks those who will learn to worship Him in spirit and in truth.

He is our awesome God, and worshiping Him leads us into realms of awe and wonder over His divine attributes. As we adore our heavenly Father, our spirit is renewed in the same way that sleep renews our bodies.

The angels are continually worshiping God, and their example is worthy to follow because it shows us the vital importance of worship: "They sing the song of Moses, the servant of God, and the song of the Lamb, saying: 'Great and marvelous are Your works, Lord God Almighty! Just and true are Your ways, O King of the saints! Who shall not fear You, O Lord, and glorify Your name? For You alone are holy, for all nations shall come and worship before You, for Your judgments have been manifested'" (Rev. 15:3-4, NKJV).

We worship God because His works are great and marvelous, His ways are true, and He is our King. He alone is holy, and through worship we glorify Him. Worship is the natural response to God when we realize that He has created us.

When Jesus went to the home of Mary and Martha He pointed out the importance of worship in our lives. Martha was scurrying about, tidying things up and preparing a meal, while her sister, Mary, was sitting at the footstool of Jesus and listening to Him. When Martha went to the Master and protested by pointing out that she was doing all the work, Jesus gently rebuked her, "Martha, Martha, thou art careful and troubled about many things: But one thing is needful: and Mary hath chosen that good part, which shall not be taken away from her" (Luke 10:41-42).

The one needful thing, "that good part," to which Jesus refers is worship and intimacy. Mary wanted, above all else, to be with Jesus and listen to His voice. It is more important than service or any other thing, because what we learn about God through worship will never be taken away from us.

No one is like our God. He alone is worthy of our worship. As one song proclaims, "Worship belongs to our God. He is a great God above all others. Worship belongs to our God."

God is incomparably worthy to receive our worship. "Thou art worthy, O Lord, to receive glory and honour and power: for thou hast created all things, and for thy pleasure they are and were created" (Rev. 4:11).

William Temple, an Anglican clergyman, wrote, "True worship is to quicken the conscience by the holiness of God, to feed the mind with the truth of God, to purge the imagination by the beauty of God, to open the heart to the love of God, to devote the will to the purpose of God. All this is gathered up in the emotion which most cleanses us from selfishness because it is the most selfless of all emotions – worship."

Worship Is Enjoying God

Worship is enjoying being with God. It is sitting at His footstool and listening for His heavenly voice.

Worship tunes our ears to hear God's voice speaking to our hearts. As we shut ourselves in with God, tuning out all other voices, and silently adoring Him, amazing things begin to happen. As Elijah stood on the mountain before the Lord God, he heard the still, small voice of God speaking to him. (See 1 Kings 19:12.) It was the voice of God telling him what to do next. In the same way, God speaks to us through worship. He gives us direction, and He gives us insight into His very nature. He also enjoys being with us and expressing His love to us.

Jonathan Edwards said, "The enjoyment of God is the only happiness with which our souls can be satisfied. To go to heaven, fully to enjoy God, is infinitely better than the most pleasant accommodations here. Fathers and mothers, husbands, wives, or children, or the company of earthly friends, are but shadows; but God is the substance. These are but scattered beams, but God is the sun. These are but streams. But God is the ocean."

Through worship, therefore, we are able to enjoy God and He is able to enjoy us. John Piper puts it this way: "The good news for those who enjoy God's being God is that He enjoys *them*. He delights in those who hope in His immeasurable power. O, may the truth grip us that God is God and that He works omnipotently for those who wait for Him (Isaiah 64:4), hope in Him (Psalm 147:11), and

love Him (Romans 8:28). He loves to be God
for the weak and childlike, who look to Him
for all they need."

Worship is waiting in God, hoping in
God, and loving Him. God seeks worshipers
who will include these qualities when they
are worshiping Him. The result will be an
immeasurable increase in our knowledge of
God, because worship is enjoying the
presence of God.

Who shall ascend into the hill of the
Lord? Or who shall stand in his
holy place? He that hath clean hands,
and a pure heart; who hath not lifted up
his soul unto vanity, nor sworn deceitfully.
(Ps. 24:3-4)

Prayer Response: Heavenly Father, thank you
for giving me the avenues of praise and
worship to help me draw closer to you. I
desire to have an intimate relationship with
you at all times, and I praise you and thank
you for all you have done and are doing in
my life, and for who you are to me. I love
you, and I thank you for loving me. In Jesus'
name, Amen.

13

KNOWING GOD THROUGH HIS CREATION AND HIS PRESENCE

The heavens declare the glory of God; and the firmament shows His handiwork.
(Ps. 19:1, NKJV)

Finding God Wherever We Are

God, by His Spirit, is omnipresent (present everywhere). We find Him in the beauty of His creation, and we can enjoy His presence anywhere we are.

God, as Paul points out, can be known through nature: "For since the creation of the world His invisible attributes are clearly seen, being understood by the things that are made, even His eternal power and Godhead, so that they are without excuse, because, although they knew God, they did not glorify Him as God, nor were thankful, but became futile in their thoughts, and their foolish hearts were darkened" (Rom. 1:20-21, NKJV).

There can be no excuse for not knowing God, because the Bible tells us that God's invisible attributes are clearly seen through His creation. All of nature proclaims the glory of God. Nature reveals God's eternal power and Majesty to us.

Often, Jesus taught to us from parables related to nature. The Parable of the Sower and Seed is one such example, and this parable serves to help us understand each of His parables. He took this parable from nature, as He did so many of His teachings.

Nature has so much to teach us about God. Predators in the animal kingdom, for example, come out at night, in the darkness, in order to destroy and kill others. This shows us that evil thrives in darkness, but it is the Light that brings peace and safety. We learn that darkness and light cannot exist together either in the physical or spiritual realm.

A mighty waterfall speaks to us of God's strength and power. A flower speaks of His purity, grace, beauty, and creativity. In the pounding of the surf on the seashore we hear His voice. As we gaze upon lofty mountain peaks, covered with snow, our hearts are lifted toward Him. The eagle soaring majestically above the peaks lets us know what God wants for us. The billowy clouds on a clear summer day help us to know peace and serenity. We can see God in all His glory revealed by dark thunderheads shooting their lightning bolts to the earth. We can be transported to wonder and worship when we see a vivid sunset painted in hues of lavender, gold, and pink across the twilight sky. Whether it is a chipmunk scampering among the rocks or a bluebird perched upon a limb, all of nature tells us God is love.

Nature draws us into wonder, contemplation, meditation, and solitude as we reflect upon God's handiwork all around us. At such times we hear God's voice saying, "Be still, and know that I am God" (Ps. 46:10).

This is experiencing the presence of God, and we can experience Him wherever we go.

A Letter From the Father to You

My child, I am the Creator of the universe.[1] I am your Creator as well.[2] Stand still, and consider all of My wondrous works.[3] The earth is filled with the riches I've created for you to enjoy.[4]

By My Word the heavens were made.[5] I simply spoke and everything was created.[6] Remember that I am the one who made you as well.[7] You are the wonderful craftsmanship of My hands.[8] I made you, and all things, for myself.[9] I created you for My glory.[10] Never forget, beloved child, that I am the Potter and you are the clay.[11]

I am continuing My workmanship in your life.[12] You continue to be the work of My hands.[13] I will continue to develop you until the image of My Son will be formed in you.[14]

Dearly beloved, be of good courage.[15] I will never leave you nor forsake you.[16] I am with you always.[17] My way is perfect, and My Word is tried. I am your shield as you learn to trust in Me.[18]

My promise is to be near you when you call upon Me in truth.[19] My Spirit is with you.[20] I dwell in your midst.[21] My child, I am your Father, and I see in secret, but I shall reward you openly.[22] I love to draw near to you as you draw near to Me.[23]

References: (1) Genesis 1; (2) Isaiah 64:8; (3) Job 37:14; (4) Psalms 104:24; (5) Psalms 33:6; (6) Psalms 33:9; (7) Psalms 100:3; (8) Isaiah 64:8; (9) Proverbs 16:4; (10) Isaiah 43:7; (11) Isaiah 64:8; (12) Ephesians 2:10; (13) Isaiah 64:8; (14) Romans 8:29; (15) Joshua 1:9; (16) Hebrews 13:5; (17) Matthew 28:20; (18) Psalms 18:30; (19) Psalms 145:18; (20) Haggai 2:5; (21) Zechariah 2:10; (22) Matthew 6:6; (23) James 4:8.

Our Father Created the Universe

Imagine what would happen if a missionary in some remote portion of the world, where the technological advancements we enjoy on a daily basis do not exist, were to accidentally drop his watch in the wilderness before returning home. It is likely that he would search diligently for it. Suppose, however, that he did not find his watch.

Continuing this hypothetical example, let's imagine that a native of the region discovered the watch. It is likely that he would pick up the shiny timepiece, examine it with his eyes, listen for its sounds, and wonder what it was supposed to do.

Even though the native would not understand the purpose of the watch, he would surely conclude that it had been designed by someone, somewhere. He might not understand its intricacies and its purposes, but he would understand that it is a beautiful object, a work of art. In all probability, he would want to keep it and show it to others.

This watch proves its maker and its designer in that it would not exist unless someone had crafted it. It also appears to have a purpose, even though the purpose might be unknown to the native. That there was a mind behind the creation of the watch is evident even to the most naïve observer.

The same is true with nature, our world, the solar system, and the universe. It is purposeful. It is beautifully designed. It is symmetrical. It had to be created by someone, and that Someone is God, our heavenly

Father. It is illogical to draw any other conclusion.

Because this is so, we can safely conclude that our God is very creative. All of nature teaches us that this is so. He is an artist, *par excellence*. His creativity is revealed in the mountains, the dales, the hills, the oceans, the moon, the sun, the birds, the animals, the flowers, and all of nature.

In the Book of Genesis we learn how God created the earth, all living creatures, the heavenly bodies, animals, vegetation, and us. From the very beginning, we see the Father's heart crying out for companionship with His children. "Then God said, 'Let Us make man in Our image, according to Our likeness; let them have dominion over the fish of the sea. . . .Then God blessed them" (Gen. 1:26-28, NKJV).

God prepared a garden for human beings to enjoy – a place where men and women could talk with Him. "Then God saw everything that He had made, and indeed it was very good" (Gen. 1:31, NKJV).

Nature Reveals God's Power

The Psalmist writes, "He commandeth, and raiseth the stormy wind, which lifteth up the waves thereof" (Ps. 107:25).

As mankind continued its downward spiral into wanton sin after the Fall of Adam and Eve, God decided to show His wrath by sending a great deluge that drowned nearly everyone. It rained for forty days and forty nights.

There was one family, however, that escaped God's wrath – the family of Noah – a righteous man, full of faith. What does this story teach us about our Father? It shows that He always rewards righteousness and faith. "But without faith it is impossible to please Him, for he who comes to God must believe that He is, and that He is a rewarder of those who diligently seek Him. By faith Noah, being divinely warned of things not yet seen, moved with godly fear, prepared an ark for the saving of his household, by which he condemned the world and became heir of the righteousness which is according to faith" (Heb. 11:6-7, NKJV).

After the Flood, God revealed His heart to us through nature again, in the form of the rainbow. "This is the sign of the covenant which I make between Me and you, and every living creature that is with you, for perpetual generations: I set My rainbow in the cloud, and it shall be for the sign of the covenant between Me and the earth. It shall be, when I bring a cloud over the earth, that the rainbow shall be seen in the cloud; and I will remember My covenant which is between Me and you and every living creature of all flesh; the waters shall never again become a flood to destroy all flesh" (Gen. 9:12-15, NKJV).

The rainbow speaks to us of God's love and His faithfulness. A covenant is a strong agreement, and it is rooted in relationship. God's rainbow-covenant with his people is a sign that He wants us to know Him, believe, Him, and trust Him.

God is the One who, ". . .coverest thyself with light as with a garment: who stretchest out the heavens like a curtain: Who layeth the beams of his chambers in the waters: who maketh the clouds his chariot: who walketh upon the wings of the wind: Who maketh his angels spirits; his ministers a flaming fire" (Ps. 104:2-4).

A Very Present Help to Us

When we feel that God has abandoned us or that He cannot hear our prayers, the problem is with us, not with God, because God is always there – in the here-and-now of our lives. He is a very present help to us no matter where we are. A friend of ours said, "As long as you see that the birds are still flying, you know that God is still working."

Sometimes when we feel discouraged, it helps a lot just to look around us and see all that God has done and is doing. We see nature alive with the life, the glory, and the power of God, and we are reminded that He is always there and always caring for us.

A title of one of Francis A. Schaeffer's books speaks volumes to us about our ever-present, ever-hearing God: *He Is There, and He Is Not Silent*. Thankfully, we can know our Father as the omnipresent (always present) God, and He has promised never to leave us or forsake us. "...For He Himself has said, 'I will never leave you nor forsake you.' So we may boldly say: 'The Lord is my helper; I will not fear. What can man do to me?'" (Heb. 13:6, NKJV).

God says, "*I will never leave you.*" We respond, "Therefore, I will not fear, because God is my Helper."

One of the names of God is *Jehovah-Shammah*, "the Lord God is present." We discover this name in the Book of Ezekiel, where the prophet is describing Zion, the city of God, the land of promise, to the Israelites: "All the way around shall be eighteen thousand cubits; and the name of the city from that day shall be: 'THE LORD IS THERE'" (Ezek. 48:35, NKJV). God dwells upon a throne in heaven, in the midst of His people, and upon the throne of our hearts. He is always with us! Joel emphasizes this truth for us: "For the Lord dwells in Zion" (Joel 3:21, NKJV).

God Is Omnipresent

Our heavenly Father is omniscient (all-knowing) and omnipotent (all-powerful). He is also omnipresent (everywhere present). This reality about our God helps us to know Him and experience Him as the One who is always there. It is this attribute of God that enables us to have fellowship with Him as we go along on our pilgrimage. The old hymn describes this relationship vividly for us:

And He walks with me,
and He talks with me,
And He tells me I am His own,
And the joy we share as we tarry there,
None other has ever known.
(From "I Come to the Garden Alone"
by C. Austin Miles)

God walks with us, and He talks with us. Our loving Father wants to have fellowship with His children, and He is ever-present in our lives, no matter where we are, to help us, cheer us, guide us, and to love us.

The omnipresence of God is closely related to His omnipotence and His omniscience. No matter where we are, therefore, He is there. This means that His power is available to us everywhere, and that He has full knowledge of everything that is happening in our life.

Jeremiah wrote: "Am I a God at hand, saith the Lord, and not a God afar off? Can any hide himself in secret places that I shall not see him? saith the Lord. Do not I fill heaven and earth? saith the Lord" (Jer. 23:23-24). Nothing can be hidden from our God, because He is Jehovah-Shammah.

The Psalmist tells us that no one can flee from the presence of God. He begins by praising the omniscience of God: "O Lord, You have searched me and known me. You know my sitting down and my rising up; You understand my thought afar off. You comprehend my path and my lying down, and are acquainted with all my ways. For there is not a word on my tongue, but behold, O Lord, You know it altogether. You have hedged me behind and before, and laid Your hand upon me. Such knowledge is too wonderful for me; it is high, I cannot attain it" (Ps. 139:1-6, NKJV). Truly, God knows everything about us.

The Psalmist proceeds to elaborate on the omnipresence of our Father as well: "Where can I go from Your Spirit? Or where can I flee from Your presence? If I ascend into heaven, You are there; if I make my bed in hell, behold You are there. If I take the wings of the morning, and dwell in the uttermost parts of the sea, even there Your hand shall lead me, and your right hand shall hold me" (Ps. 139:7-10, NKJV). God is always there; He is leading us. He is holding us in His right hand.

God knows everything about us. The knowledge, power, and presence of God are always with us. "For in him we live, and move, and have our being" (Acts 17:28).

God's Presence Gives Us Comfort

Almighty God, our everlasting Father, is not only with us; He is *in* us. This fact changes everything in our lives, including given circumstances, even tragedies, we may have to go through. His comforting presence is always there. John wrote, "You are of God, little children, and have overcome them, because He who is in you is greater than he who is in the world" (1 John 4:4, NKJV).

God is always near. Faber writes, "God is never so far off, as even to be near; He is within. Our spirit is the home He holds most dear. To think of Him as by our side is almost as untrue, as to remove His shrine beyond those skies of starry blue."

God is a very present help to us. Knowing that He is near brings great peace, comfort, and hope to us. Experiencing His presence is a divinely ordered pathway to knowing God both personally and intimately.

St. Augustine ties in the omnipresence of God with our knowing Him: "The difference between knowing God in the full-orbed glow of His presence and living in the half-light of an unsatisfactory Christian experience is that important factor of spiritual receptivity – or call it spiritual response. Oh! That I might repose on Thee. Oh! That Thou wouldst enter into my heart, and inebriate it, that I may forget my ills, and embrace Thee, my sole good."

"Draw near to God and He will draw near to you" (James 4:8, NKJV).

Again, St. Augustine helps us to see what intimacy with God is really like: "Thou has made us for Thyself, O Lord, and our hearts are restless till they rest in Thee." Knowing God intimately is resting in Him, experiencing His presence, and enjoying His company. He is the greater One who lives within us.

*Serve the Lord with gladness; come
before His presence with singing. Know
that the Lord, He is God; it is He who
has made us, and not we ourselves;
we are His people and the sheep of
His pasture. Enter into His gates with
thanksgiving, and into His courts
with praise. Be thankful to Him,
and bless His name. For the Lord
is good; His mercy is everlasting, and
His truth endures to all generations.*
(Ps. 100:2-5, NKJV)

Prayer Response: Mighty God, my Creator, and my Father, I thank you for the beauty and glory of nature which reveal so much about you. Thank you for giving me life, and so many things to enjoy. Everywhere I look I see your hand at work, and when I am enjoying the beauty of your creation, I always want to draw closer to you. Thank you for walking and talking with me wherever I go. In Jesus' name, Amen.

Study Guide Now Available

A great resource for personal devotions, Sunday school classes, Bible study groups, spiritual enrichment, and anyone desiring a study aid for *Knowing God Intimately*.

For information call Victory House at:

(918) 747-5009